WHEN WE GET IT WRONG

Dominic Smart breathes some fresh air into our Christian discipleship. Here Christ himself is at the centre and grace is the first item on the agenda. *When We Get it Wrong* helps us grasp why the gentleness and ruthless commitment of Christ's love belong together. Just the book we need to strip bare the soul and recalibrate our Christian lives.

Sinclair B. Ferguson, Minister, St George's-Tron Church, Glasgow

Many books on discipleship are little more than 'how to' manuals that are seriously cut off from biblical theology. This is not one of them. Dominic Smart's highly readable volume goes after the basics. And the basics, his readers will discover, not only enable serious Christians to think about discipleship in a biblically faithful way, but focus wonderful attention on Jesus Christ himself. This will start us off on the right foot, and contribute to a lifetime of discovering what it means to confess Jesus as Lord.

Don A. Carson, Research Professor of New Testament,
Trinity Evangelical Divinity School

As I read *When We Get it Wrong*, I felt as if I was in my favourite armchair, sitting by a blazing wood fire, listening to Dominic open the Word and share from his heart. Through these warming truths from the life of Peter, I was ministered to, encouraged and blessed. I could have 'listened' all night. Draw up a chair, read and enjoy, and you will know exactly what I mean.

Roger Carswell, Evangelist, Association of Evangelists

If you have ever acted without thinking, ever blown it big time, if you are a person with a record of failure, you will identify with the big fisherman of Galilee. From spectacular crash to powerful servant, the story of Peter offers hope of forgiveness and renewed usefulness to all those who have got it wrong in their Christian life. Watch how Jesus takes this 'humpty-dumpty' of a man and put him back together again. Dominic Smart writes with typical clarity, compassion and good humour of the downs and ups of the patron saint of failure.

Liam Goligher, Senior Minister, Duke Street Church, Richmond

Just when I thought I'd read all the angles on discipleship, along comes Dominic Smart with a fresh approach. This book rocked me back on my heels, brought me down to my knees and set me up on my feet to love and follow Christ with fresh understanding and renewed zeal. Only read if you're prepared to be challenged and changed.

Alistair Begg, Senior Minister, Parkside Community Church, Ohio

I know of no other comparable book which begins with such emancipating Christology applied to the practicalities of present day discipleship.

Dennis Lennon, formerly Bishop's Advisor in Evangelism,
Diocese of Sheffield

WHEN WE GET IT WRONG

*Peter, Christ, and
a path through failure*

DOMINIC SMART

CHRISTIAN
FOCUS

Copyright © 2001 Dominic Smart

ISBN 978-1-5271-0409-9

First published in 2001 by Paternoster Lifestyle
Reprinted 2003 by Authentic Lifestyle

This edition published in 2019
by
Christian Focus Publications Ltd,
Geanies House, Fearn, Ross-shire,
IV20 1TW, Scotland, Great Britain

The right of Dominic Smart to be identified as the Author of this Work
has been asserted by him in accordance with the Copyright, Designs and
Patents Act 1988

A catalogue record for this book is available from the British Library

Cover design by Pete Barnsley
(Creativehoot.com)

Printed and Bound by
Bell & Bain, Glasgow

Contents

Acknowledgements

Thanks are due to Scripture Union Scotland who invited me to give a series of talks to new Reachout workers at their centre in Altnacriche near Aviemore. From them came the initial encouragement to go to write this book.

At a conference of the Crieff Fellowship my dear friend Sandy Tait introduced me to David Hazard. David's like-mindedness, fellowship and enthusiasm for the project sustained me when otherwise I would have given up. It was immensely stimulating to share together the theological concerns behind the book, and see their relevance for so many aspects of the Christian life. He made many useful suggestions and were it not for him, this book would never have been written.

The staff at Paternoster have been understanding, prompt, cheerful and a pleasure to get to know. They have instilled the confidence to press on at every turn.

Via conference addresses and the telephone, Dennis Lennon has been a great help. Some of the insights here were crystallised by Dennis; his address to the Evangelical Missionary Alliance on 'The Community of Possibility' saved this minister at a very low period.

Many others have contributed directly and indirectly, not least the congregations here at Gilcomston in Aberdeen and at Logie and St John's (Cross) Church in Dundee. As ever, it is my wife Marjorie, and our children, who have con-

stantly made the most significant, startling and happy con-
tributions to my life. Some of them are woven into these
chapters.

   To all I give my thanks, and for all I thank God.

Aberdeen, September 2000

1

Discipleship in Christ?

A light, airy seminar room in the Scottish Highlands. Late summer. In front of me were nine young adults. Scots, English and Russian; male, female; graduates, students. Wide ranges of tastes, personality types, expectations and gifts were to emerge during the following days of fellowship and learning. This sample of young, committed Christian adulthood was about to embark on a year of church work for Scripture Union and I had been asked to speak to them for a week (with breaks!) on discipleship.

I felt for them. Not only did they have to listen to my accent, but within a fortnight they were to be catapulted out of their comfort-zones and into a proving ground. Ahead of them lay many trials for their good, as well as many temptations for their ill. They would see God wonderfully answer their prayers and also make huge demands on them.

How well equipped were they? My concern for them had nothing to do with their ability to organise and lead exciting after-school clubs for primary children, or to stand in front of concerned parents and reassure them that Scripture Union camps are safe. I was concerned for how they would handle failure.

I didn't wish failure upon them of course, nor did I want to take a defeatist approach to following Christ. Instead I wondered how they would understand what was happening between them and God should they do what all the rest of us do: fail him.

How would they handle it, and much more importantly, how would their Saviour, Lord and Friend handle it? What would it do to their relationship and fellowship with him? How would they recover?

Were they theologically equipped to read their situation aright? There seemed then to be little in the way of books on discipleship that dealt with it going wrong. There were a few autobiographical works around, mostly helpful; but there seemed to be little in the mainstream of Christian reading, of the type that these folk had dipped into, to prepare them for the times when the disciple meets with failure.

Well, I took it as my task to help in that regard; to show them how the Bible prepares them for understanding both failure and recovery. To do so would require that we explore two areas of biblical teaching about living the Christian life. They are inseparable, like the two parts of a heartbeat. I fear that nowadays they are also largely forgotten or not even taught in the first place. The first area concerns one of the most basic questions of all for a disciple of Christ: what it is to be a Christian. Get that skewed and the rest will never make sense. The second concerns the reason for being a disciple; again, get that wrong early on in life and profound anguish almost certainly lies ahead.

We took as our guide parts of the story of Simon Peter who, in denying Christ, suffered a near-catastrophic col-

lapse. It was simultaneously the breaking and the making of
him and, astonishingly to our minds, simultaneously against
God but also within the sovereign will of the one he
denied.

The chapters that follow are based closely on the teaching given that week. I have tried to preserve some of the
immediacy of the spoken form, whilst eliminating some of
the muddles of the spoken word that are horrifyingly obvious in an unaltered transcript. This chapter is by way of a
slip road onto the main highway that we will travel with
Peter and Christ. Just as tarmac is common to the slip road
and the highway, there will necessarily and intentionally be
some material common to both this chapter and the
remainder of the book. Here, I want very briefly to open up
the two theological concerns to which I've just referred, and
hope thereby to restore us to an almost forgotten understanding of discipleship, and the helpfulness of Simon Peter's
example.

What it is to be a Christian

There is no shortage of ways to understand what it is to be
a Christian. In terms of our culture, to be a Christian is to
be politically incorrect. We believe in one who declared
himself categorically to be the way, the truth and the life
and who stated that there was no other way to God except
through him. We are immediately set at odds with the prevailing western postmodernity that says that there are many
truths and that the truthfulness of a statement is relative to

the person who hears it: 'That's true for you, but not true
for me.' Our acceptance of a big story, a 'metanarrative'
which is God's meaningful revelation of himself in his word,
marks us out as naïve and anachronistic when the new cultural norm is one of sophisticated and self-conscious
incredulity. We commit the cardinal cultural sin of intoler-
ance. We live in ways that our colleagues at work, or those
with whom we relax or study, find strange and uninviting.
Mark Greene, in his excellent book *Thank God it's Monday*,
writes of how Christians are perceived by today's non-
Christians:

> They don't dance. They don't swear. They pretend not to have
> sex. They don't know how to have fun so they ruin it for the
> rest of us. They give away their money and they go to Church
> on Sundays as if it were a social club. Frankly, my golf club is
> more fun. And it's cheaper. The whole thing is a crutch. How
> can anyone believe that stuff? It's superstitious mumbo-jumbo.
> What's worse is they're constantly trying to stuff it down our
> throats. Why should I accept it – I don't see any difference in
> their lives …[1]

Before he became a Christian, he saw Christians as 'A hud-
dle of mushy, simple-minded, ineffectual, well-meaning,
boring, hypocritical, weird people.'[2]

What it is to be a Christian is also well-defined for most
of us by the behaviour of our group. Apart from the sup-

[1] Greene, Mark, *Thank God it's Monday*, Scripture Union,
London, 1977, p 45
[2] Ibid

posedly common do's and don'ts regarding money, drugs, drink, sex and a few other aspects of life, being a Christian becomes a matter of conforming to the behavioural expectations of the Christian group that we're in (unless you're the type who sees an expectation coming a mile off and takes it as a matter of Christian obedience to defy it). The kind of clothes that you wear, Bible that you carry (or don't), music that you worship with, jargon that you use (or don't), car that you drive, dog that you walk — these and many other behavioural choices are largely shaped by what's acceptable within the group. If you want to stick out like a sore thumb and have your Christianity called into question, try offering the wrong drink to fellow Christian group members as they arrive at your house. (For some groups this would require you to offer a Harvey Wallbanger, for others, tea.) Definitions might vary, but the group does much of the defining. Even if we shun the ghetto mentality and resist the pressure to conform to a Christian group, we tend just to take on the form of that bit of the world that we inhabit. This is because we are ecological animals who need to find our place in a web of relationships.

Unfortunately, too many of our ideas about what it is to be a Christian are formed either in reaction to our culture or in conformity to the behavioural norms of our group. These two sources of 'word' sound loud and clear through each day and week. They shout to us from the media, our workplace, our churches and books. They can appeal with great plausibility to our ambitions, prejudices, fears, pride and insecurities. They have their place without doubt, but theirs ought not to be the most important voice in defining what it is to be a Christian, for neither of them speak of what we are, in our being. Neither of them say anything that is constitutive of our existence. Neither necessarily say anything about our relationship and fellowship with Christ. Unless we have been blessed with exceptionally good mentors, these closely combined voices of culture and social group give us little, and at best ambiguous, help in understanding the nature of Christian discipleship.

What does the word of God say? The Bible most frequently and foundationally expresses what it is to be a Christian in a way that we find difficult to understand immediately. We often pass over it quickly as we hasten on to the more accessible, but ultimately far less helpful, voices of secular culture and Christian sub-culture. To be a Christian is to be 'in Christ'.

The term 'in Christ' is the normal way of talking about Christian being and existence in the New Testament. The word 'Christian(s)' occurs three times (Acts 11:26; 26:28 and 1 Pet. 4:16). 'In Christ' is used no fewer than 115 times. It's a stunning list of verses which takes us into the heart of who we are, whom we serve, and what we have. (I have included a list of references at the back of this book of instances where the phrases 'in Christ' and its equivalents 'in me', 'in him', 'in the Lord' and 'in whom' occur. I have only included those verses which refer to our being and our existence, over against, for example, placing one's faith 'in Christ'. If you are ever called to preach or lead a Bible study, you'll find about five years' worth of material there. There are other, relevant passages, such as Colossians 3:1-4, which do not use the exact phrase but which refer to the same thing.)

It's not my aim to explore all the nuances of these references here. I simply want to establish that as far as the word of God is concerned, what it is to be a Christian is defined as 'being in'. It's a phrase that is strange to modern ears – 'being in'. It's borrowed not just from the theologians, but also from Scripture. (How happy it is when the two coincide!) On Mars Hill in Athens, Paul redefined the view of man for his sophisticated audience when he took the root of our being out of the soil of human philosophy, out of the cultural and behavioural earth, and re-rooted it in God himself. He said, 'In him we live and move and have our being.' Humanity is defined with reference to God who, as Paul proclaimed to the Athenians, gives us breath, determines our lives, is not far from us, claims repentance from us and will judge us (Acts 17:22ff.).

For the Christian, our new nature, our being, what it means to be human, are all grounded in Christ. Follow through the list of references at the back of the book and you'll see how that small preposition proclaims volumes of theology. We are saved not only *by* Christ, but *in* Christ. Not only did he die *for* us, but we also died *with* him. Not only did he rise for us, but we also rise *in* him. Thus there is no end to sin and its power or guilt other than that end of it which Christ made on the cross and rising from the tomb. There is no eternal life that we produce – we only have it in him. There is no holiness save that which is his and becomes ours by virtue of our union with him – becomes ours, as the Puritans taught, by imputation (*his* holiness is attributed to us) and impartation (that is, it is made our experience as the years go by and as we grow as Christians). There is no righteousness save that which has appeared from God – in Christ. And so we could go on. There is no being a Christian that isn't 'being in Christ'.

All this is inseparable from the presentation in the Bible of Christ as what Luther called the 'Proper Man'. All that the Father should rightly receive from those whom he made, he has only received from his Son whom he sent. But he received it from Christ who became one of us, the Son of Man, and so received it from him on behalf of us. I have no goodness to bring to God which is my own, but there is one – my Brother – who has been able to offer perfect goodness on my behalf.

Christ's union with us in all our humanity, fallen under the curse of God, and our union with him in all his humanity, spotless, righteous and risen, defines us. It, and it alone, is the given basis for our discipleship. It alone defines for us the important elements in our walk with him.

Therefore a staggeringly different view of discipleship emerges. It is this: my discipleship (all my repentance, obedience, service, action, praying, you name it), seen as an offering to the Father, is acceptable because I am 'in Christ' who has already 'done' discipleship for me, and done it perfectly. He has already offered unalloyed repentance (see his baptism for repentance – Mt. 3:11ff. and parallel passages in Mk. 1:4 and Lk. 3:3), perfect obedience (see Phil. 2:6-11) and uncompromised service (see the four Servant Songs in Is. chapters 42, 49, 50 and 52-53). As our representative (our 'champion' in the old sense of the word – one who fights victoriously for us not over us!) he has already perfectly offered godly action, fervent and acceptable praying and all the rest.

This is the theological understanding, given to us in God's word, of what it means to be a Christian and therefore a disciple. Our walk with Christ has a context: that of being in Christ, in whom all that I have and am, and all that I will be for God, is acceptable because of the perfect Son in whom I have my entire being. All my repentance, my service and my offerings are accepted not because they are good enough for a holy God, nor because God drops his standards. (God cannot drop his standards because they are the reflection of his glory.) They are accepted and pleasing to God because I bring them in and through the Lord Jesus Christ, and can bring them no other way. By the same token, my repentance, service and offerings of time, talents and money are not rejected because they are sub-standard, but rather accepted because I bring them in Christ in whom they are made right. In Christ I have reason neither to be proud and boastful, nor despairing of my uselessness for always falling short of his mark. We are, on the one hand, God's workmanship created in Christ, so that there is no room for boasting (see Eph. 2:10) and on the other, assured that our labour in the Lord is not in vain (see 1 Cor. 15:58). Being a disciple then, is a matter of being in Christ, who has been for us (if we may adapt Luther's phrase) the Proper Disciple.

The End of Legalism

Since the context for my discipleship is being in Christ, the prevailing view of the chief practices and duties of a disciple must change. It seems to me that the pragmatism of our age, with its clamour for usefulness and practicality, has created a false view of what is important for a disciple of Christ. There has grown up a subject area called discipleship – it has seeded our bookshelves with a host of 'how to' manuals which tell us what we must do and how to do it best. It promises a harvest of effective and enjoyable Christianity. Now there is nothing about the scriptural context for understanding what it is to be a Christian which suggests that practice is unnecessary, nor that good practice is somehow not to be aimed at, nor that misery is virtuous; but the great danger of putting what I do before what I am – of approaching the practicalities of Christian living apart from the context of Christian being – is that I succumb to the essentially legalistic pressure of the flesh.

What do I mean? By using the term legalism here I do not mean the habit of surrounding all practice with rules (do this, don't do that; no TV on Tuesdays; you must come to the Bible study at least three weeks out of four; you must never drink alcohol and always go on a mission in the summer; if you're female, wear a hat to church, etc). Undoubtedly this couches much of the Christian life in the terminology of laws, but it's not the heart of legalism and it certainly doesn't appeal to the flesh. (Most people's flesh just wants to get on with what it wants to do and certainly doesn't want to have its style cramped by a load of party-pooping rules!)

The heart of legalism is an attitude: 'I *can* make myself acceptable to God by what I do.' It is self-realising, instead of accepting the realisation of our lives in Christ. It is works mad, because it knows nothing of the rest that comes through faith in Christ. It panders to our activist natures – those who are energetic and well-organised can be especially susceptible to its poisonous charms. It is alien to grace and mercy. It is of the flesh, not the Spirit. It substitutes the word of God for the traditions of men. It was legalism that lay at the heart of the Pharisees' quizzing of Christ over his disciples' conduct. The Pharisees put their rules, the keeping of which was supposed to pave a path to righteousness, before the word of God. (Read Mk. 7:1-13 for Jesus' razor-sharp treatment of the Pharisees on this issue.)

Of course, very few of us would ever say that we are legalistic. But it is the practical approach to the Christian life that is all too commonly pressed upon us in our churches and fellowships, even though it is never articulated as such. The approach has a rationale which goes something like this. As far as my conversion was concerned, that was a matter of God's grace. We aren't saved by anything that we have done; in fact we could do nothing to merit forgiveness even if we were given all the Sundays that there will ever be. We might not be too sure about exactly where free will, our repentance and the sovereignty of God come into it, but we're pretty sure that we are saved not because we deserve it but because God loves us. But then, once saved, it's a different matter. Now we can, no, we *must* do those things which can (so we think) ensure our continuing acceptability to God. We were initially accepted by God on the basis of his love for us, but now, being capable of doing good, we must maintain our acceptability by keeping the good works tally high. In slightly more theological language, we were justified by God's grace through faith in Christ, but practically speaking we think and act as if we are sanctified by pulling ourselves up by our own boot straps. We thus come to God (in worship, service, discipleship – falsely so-called) on the basis of our works for God and not on the basis of God's abiding work for us in Christ. Isn't that how it goes?

Thus we set sail on a vast swamp of troubles. Acceptance becomes a matter of performance appraisal; therefore assurance goes right out of the window. How can we ever know that we've done well enough? Or else assurance becomes the expression of our arrogance and pride because we actually think that we *have* done well enough. Jesus' amazing invitation in Matthew 11:28, which should be such a relief to us, becomes an impossible burden; as if Jesus said: 'Come to me all you who labour and are heavy laden, and I will give you ... a treadmill!' Discipleship becomes a specialised course in the University of Legalistic Living.

What does this kind of approach to being a disciple of Christ look like in practice? Well, it has at least three features. First, it becomes task-oriented, rather than relationship-oriented. The tasks we undertake for God in that corner of existence known as Christian service become more important than the quality of our relationship and fellowship with him. Second, the 'energy' is all the wrong way round. Instead of being motivated by love, we become motivated by the wrong sort of fear – akin to insecurity. Christian work becomes draining instead of joy-giving. The reward for doing work well is uneasily hoped for instead of the work being its own reward. Those in 'full-time Christian work' ('salaried Christians' among whom I was included the other day – yugh!) easily overwork, afraid of failing to reach the standard. We behave like those who are driven rather than those who are called. Third, we develop, in our task-oriented sub-culture, a hectic life that is split three ways: the life of Christian work, the life of secular work and family. Rarely do the demands of each coincide to build us up in our faith; usually they form a kind of spiritual Bermuda Triangle, in which our Christian being disappears off the radar screen. Fearing that we might not make the grade in all departments, we ricochet off the incessant demands of each. Sincere, conscientious, promising Christians suffer most.

In this Christian world, 'discipleship' becomes one of those words that makes anyone who has an ounce of normality still functioning within them groan. Rightly so. Keen, bright-eyed, I've-got-my-act-together, 'successful' Christians are good at it; but it makes them intimidating or nauseating, unpleasant to live or work with. The rest of us, particularly if we're putting a bit of weight on already, will probably fail. On this line, 'discipleship' is not life, it's an added extra, like the turbocharger unit put in the engines of cars that most of us will never afford.

'Being in Christ' rescues us from this swamp of legalistic discipleship. First, you can rest in Christ – in fact must rest in him. Of course his burden feels light to us! It is his burden, and though we now carry it with him, he does not need our help. It's rather like a felled tree being carried by an elephant and a flea. Overworked Christians can take a day off. Second, you can come to God without insecurity, and with precisely the kind of confidence and boldness that he has told us he wants to see – the fruits of security in Christ, who is our sanctification and the new and living way into the presence of God. Third, we avoid the compartmentalised life in which God is only really interested in the religious compartments. All life is embraced and redeemed by God. I am in Christ in the office, taking the kids to school, waiting in the doctor's surgery, at the supermarket, putting the business plan to the bank manager, on holiday, signed off with depression, at the Bible study. Your whole life is in him and for him. Not just the religious bits. Music, the visual arts, the imagination, windsurfing, cooking, volleyball, basket-weaving (though possibly not the mud-wrestling) – your whole life is discipleship in him and for him. And most crucially, in all these aspects of your life, in your 'whole discipleship', your communion with him becomes more important than your operational efficiency. Jesus gave the disciples remarkably little to do. Their main calling was simply to be with him and learn from him. In the Son, I live my whole life also as a son or daughter of the Father, not as an operative in a deity's factory. Which means, of course, that when I fail, I fail him who loves me, which makes it both more hurtful and, praise God, more hopeful, for I do not face the sack. Which brings us, at last, to Peter the fisherman.

2

The Disciple's call

Luke 5:1-11

1 One day as Jesus was standing by the Lake of Gennesaret, with the people crowding round him and listening to the word of God, 2 he saw at the water's edge two boats, left there by the fishermen, who were washing their nets.

3 He got into one of the boats, the one belonging to Simon, and asked him to put out a little from shore. Then he sat down and taught the people from the boat.

4 When he had finished speaking, he said to Simon, "Put out into deep water, and let down the nets for a catch."

5 Simon answered, "Master, we've worked hard all night and haven't caught anything. But because you say so, I will let down the nets."

6 When they had done so, they caught such a large number of fish that their nets began to break.

7 So they signalled to their partners in the other boat to come and help them, and they came and filled both boats so full that they began to sink.

8 When Simon Peter saw this, he fell at Jesus' knees and said, "Go away from me, Lord; I am a sinful man!"

9 For he and all his companions were astonished at the catch of fish they had taken,

10 and so were James and John, the sons of Zebedee, Simon's partners. Then Jesus said to Simon, "Don't be afraid; from now on you will catch men."

11 So they pulled their boats up on shore, left everything and followed him.

These verses describe a scene for us which, for all its extraordinary and divine events, is painted on a very human canvas. The disciples have been fishing all night. It's some time during the morning; they are mending their nets, doubtless bemoaning a lousy night's fishing, looking forward to breakfast and a little sleep. The sun is shining; the water laps gently on the shore, but these experienced, professional fishermen, whose livelihood depends on their successful catching of fish, have just got it wrong. They are weary.

However, despite the momentary difficulty, their lives are generally good. Life is regular and well-ordered. They get up, go out and fish, usually catch some, come back to the shore, deal with the fish and mend their nets. Their wives or mothers cook breakfast or supper. Life is fairly well-ordered. There is a predictable pattern: they know what tomorrow is going to be like, weather permitting.

Their identity – what they think of themselves – is so clearly established that it never really gets thought about any more. These are ordinary working men. Peter and James and John don't go in for profound philosophical discussions about their psyche or their ego or their id. They've stopped asking 'Who am I?' questions some time ago: everybody and everything tells them who they are – 'You're Simon. You're a fisherman. You go out and fish, when you've caught enough, you bring them home and mend the nets … that's who you are.' Simon, like most men there, knows where he fits in in society. He knows what other people's expectations of him are. His identity is like one of those stones at the bottom of the wall: he'd no more think about asking questions about who or what he is than you would think about pulling such a stone out again to see if it's okay. He knows who he is and what he's here for.

Simon, like James and John, the sons of Zebedee, his part-ners, and like the other fishermen who work the Sea of Galilee, is looking after himself. He has a business to run and a family to feed and clothe. He is nobody's servant – he has his co-workers of course, but they share that common lack of accountability. Nobody is checking up on them or audit-ing their performance. Like everyone else, they live quietly, innocently and simply for themselves.

Then, unannounced, came Jesus. Along came Jesus and a huge crowd. Well, it was unusual for that to happen. It was unusual for a huge crowd to be listening. We know that the reputation that the Rabbis had in the synagogue was not good, but unlike the hypocrites who taught in the syna-gogue, Jesus amazed people because he taught with an authenticity that lent compelling authority to everything that he said. He taught in a way that people could under-stand. He was able to identify with people in the way that he spoke to them. The crowd enjoyed the way that Jesus came out from behind the professional cleric's mask and tore down the pretence of the Pharisees and Scribes and all the rest of them. They recognised somebody who understood them, and who spoke about things that they could understand. He spoke about fish, about farming, about birds and flowers growing. They might not have understood what all this had to do with God, or what it had to do with Jesus personally, nor did they comprehend the impact that it should have had on their lives; but he didn't dazzle them with great long words; he didn't ask them weird questions about their epistemology; he just spoke to them in language that they could understand. He could relax and eat with them. He even had a sense of humour.

A huge crowd follows Jesus along the shore, listening to this maverick teacher with a reputation. There are so many people that Jesus has to step back from them. He also wants to make sure that they're not crowded so close to him that the ones five rows back can't hear a thing. He wants to teach them from the position of authority, which is sitting down, but he doesn't want to be pushed into the lake. So he climbs into a boat.

Already a storm is beginning to brew. Soon it will break on Simon's head. There were two boats, but Jesus didn't just go for the closest. He knew that moment was drawing close when he was going to reach out to Simon and draw him to be a disciple. Something had to happen in his life on that day after the fruitless night's fishing, and it could only happen in Simon's boat.

What's going on here? Even though it's written in terms that might suggest that things are unfolding in a fairly unplanned way, what's actually taking place is a meticulously planned event, timed to perfection. Jesus knows exactly what he has to do. This is no 'happenstance', no fortuitous circumstance. This is an organised moment on which would turn the whole of Simon's life. He doesn't know that: nobody knows except the one man who has to make it all happen: Jesus.

Jesus climbs into Simon's boat and continues teaching until he's finished. He does not do as he often does elsewhere: he does not dismiss the crowd. We must assume that the crowd is still there watching him. (Maybe they are waiting for the question sheets so that they can break into small groups and discuss what he's just said!) Jesus ignores them. He turns to Simon and right out-of-the-blue says to him: 'Put out into the deep water and let down your nets for a catch.' You can picture the reaction. 'Who does he think he is? This man is a carpenter-turned-Rabbi; worse, he comes from Nazareth – can anything good come from Nazareth? Who is he to tell us professional fishermen what to do? We know this lake like the back of our hands. We know fishing, and we're not going to have some popular religious teacher telling us what to do with our boats and nets, thank you.' But there is something in Jesus; was it in his face, or his voice? Jesus taught with authority. There was something compelling about his personality. Whatever it was Simon could not resist: 'Master, we've been fishing all night and haven't caught a thing, but (and implicitly it's 'just because you say so') I'll do the one thing that, as a tired and professional fisherman, I don't want to do. Simply because you say so, I'm going to do it. I'll let down the nets.' There is a huge catch of fish.

There is something vital to take account of here – it will echo again in the remaining chapters. You and I need to understand and take this to heart. It concerns our friend and leader, our Master and the one whom we are serving throughout our discipleship. He meets the fishermen – and Simon in particular – at the point of their failure. His wonderful, inspired collision with Simon is right at the point where Peter has experienced something that all of us will experience at some time or another: futile toil. When we think that we've worked hard and it's all been for nothing; when we doubt our competence (for good reasons: there weren't any fish!); when we feel a little bit embarrassed (you can imagine what all the other blokes said when they came out of their beds that morning); when we may be feeling that we're going into one of those slumps that we sink into – it's right at that point, the point where all our toil seems futile, and we perceive ourselves as failures, where Jesus meets Simon and completely transforms his life.

We sometimes think that Jesus is really close to us when we're being successful, when everything is going well, when we're on some kind of 'roll'. 'Lord, because you are so thrilled with me, you must be right by me now. This is wonderful, Jesus and me! This really is the best combination, this really is how it should be.' We miss the point that when Jesus reached out and lifted Simon Peter's life onto a completely different level, transforming his life for ever, he met him at the point of futile, profitless toil, tiredness and inevitable self-doubt. The point where you feel lowest and most useless, the point where you find yourself praying 'Lord, get me out of the way will you?', is precisely the point where Jesus reaches out to you and begins to lift your life and transform your service, opening your eyes to the wonderful truth that the best thing we can bring to God is a pair of empty hands. 'Here I am Lord. I'm not much good at this. I know that you've given me gifts and abilities, but I'm really not even very good at using those.'

The notion of seriously calling oneself a 'profitless servant' might be ridiculed as belonging to the past, or to a false, sanctimonious jargon-laden piety. Our self-image boosting, therapy-oriented Christianity has supposedly out-grown such blatant claptrap. We might rightly react against such false, self-denigrating lowliness, that prides itself on ever more grovelling expressions of humility, but in doing so we might inadvertently throw out a biblical baby with the unctuous bath-water. Who are those whom Jesus prom-ised will see God, and therefore are described by him as blessed – complete, happy; in the colloquial language of the north-west of England, 'made-up'? Those who are poor in spirit – who are, and know they are, spiritually bankrupt. No capital with which to buy favour with God; no bargaining power, no resources of their own that they can muster against the foe.

Nothing in my hand I bring, Simply to Thy cross I cling,

wrote Toplady in his hymn *Rock of Ages*. Christina Rossetti wrote:

None other Lamb, none other Name,
None other Hope in heaven or earth or sea,
None other Hiding-place from guilt and shame,
None beside Thee.

'Profitless servant' is the authentic attitude of those who, having a sober estimate of their faith, recognise their poverty of spirit. Jesus prized this attitude. He responded to brokenness and weakness; as Simon Peter would later rediscover.

So, Simon throws the net out on the other side and there is such a large number of fish that their nets began to break – a fantastically, lavishly large catch of fish, completely over-the-top. (A very lucrative catch too: the businessmen would have been well impressed with this.) Jesus didn't need to provide that many fish: one would have been better than Simon and his colleagues.

The storm-clouds have been gathering with greater and greater foreboding. Now they break. When the fish come in, Simon's world is completely shattered. His normal existence, his well-ordered routine, his quiet, regular life, his unquestioned identity – all are suddenly changed. It is a whirlwind that screams through Simon's life.

Look at the details of Peter's response. The immediate reflex is to call the others over to help – they had to stop the boat from sinking. But then the impact of what has happened hits Simon. Sometimes we go onto auto-pilot and don't realise what's happening until a few moments later. Well, Simon goes onto the fisherman's auto-pilot and fills the boats so that they don't sink. But then it strikes him, then he feels the impact. It's as if Jesus, with no religious language, with very few words of any description, by his simple presence and the effortless exercise of sovereign power, has ruined the jigsaw of Simon's life. For years, Simon has been busy piecing it together. He thought he'd got it into fairly good shape. In that moment Jesus throws the whole thing up into the air and the pieces fall down into the   bottom of the boat, in among the miraculous fish, in the most hopeless mess. Except, of course, that it's not hopeless. Jesus is going to spend the rest of his ministry, and beyond then by the Spirit, the rest of Simon's life, putting the pieces back together until, on the face an ordinary fisherman, they make the very image of God.

Why is it an event that causes such turmoil for him? Again, look at the detail. In that moment, he sees more than the amazing catch. His eyes are opened to the Catcher – to the man who's standing there in the boat with him. The good teacher, probably a good carpenter too, turns out to be a good fisherman as well. All of a sudden Simon's eyes are opened to the real identity of the man standing there. Instantly his perception of Jesus changes. Some of the disciples took a lot more time to see this. For Peter it was a quantum leap. Notice how he addressed him in v.5: 'Simon answered "Master, we have worked hard all night."' 'Master.' He was a teacher, a man you'd speak to with respect – Master. Now look at what he calls him in v.8: 'Lord.' There is a world of difference between the Master of v.5 and the Lord of v.8. Lord is sometimes just another word for Sir in the New Testament, but Lord is Luke's favourite title for Christ. It's something that Peter wouldn't have called anyone else. 'Lord' identifies something of the divinity of this person. 'This person is the one we've been waiting for, the one that we're supposed to worship and bow down to. This is God. We've been taught since we were knee-high-to-a-grasshopper that Jehovah's Anointed One was coming, and all of a sudden he's standing here in my boat!' Simon Peter clearly recognises, when he calls him Lord, that this is God in human flesh. Simon hasn't gone to theology school. He hasn't read thick tomes on the incarnation. Simon wouldn't know academic Christology if it landed in his fish soup. But he recognises the man as God. And he falls down before him.

This is the starting-point for authentic discipleship – Christ invades and interrupts our world. More or less spectacularly, suddenly or over a while, he reveals to our once-blind eyes his true identity. We fall at his feet. Sadly, it's also the point of departure from authentic discipleship as other visions of this world fill our horizons. 'Demas has left me, because he loved this world,' wrote Paul to Timothy. He chose another way.

Why does he fall down, instead of dancing with delight that Jesus was in his boat and there were more fish than he could count? Because Peter doesn't just see Jesus in a new way. Jesus is transformed from being the teacher or the Master to being the Lord; but also, crucially, Simon's view of himself is transformed. He sees himself in a different way. The world 'out there' has certainly changed; but the world 'in here' has changed too. This respectable, fine, decent, law-abiding grown man falls at Jesus' knees and says: 'Go away from me Lord, for I am a sinful man.' Not 'I'm a useless fisherman,' but 'I am a sinful man.' Suddenly his identity is defined in terms of how he relates to this man next to him in the boat. Suddenly, and for the rest of his life, his identity has to do not with his work, nor with his family relations, nor with where he comes from, nor with his accent; his view of himself doesn't have anything to do with how much he can earn, with his looks, or the quality of his clothes. Suddenly his identity has nothing to do with the things by which we are tempted to define our identities. Now his identity has to do with how he stands in relation to this God: he is a sinful man.

That's all he can say about himself. Absolute poverty of spirit. He sees that he has no bargaining power or negotiating leverage with this Lord. He can't say 'I'm a sinful man, but I'm not a bad fisherman.' He can't appeal to being a decent sort of chap or an honest businessman. He can't say 'I'm a sinful man, but …' There are no qualifications which will lessen his sinfulness; no mitigating circumstances. His whole identity is suddenly opened up to him as being sinful. 'Go away from me Lord. I am a sinful man.'

It's not just sins either. Not just 'You know I've been a bit naughty.' ('You know what I was thinking about during that Bible study last night', or 'You know what I said when I stubbed my toe last Thursday', or 'You know that I should have given more of that money away.') It's not just sinful deeds done by an otherwise righteous man. It is his whole being. At the centre of what it means to be Simon is something drastically wrong. There is a holy terror – 'Go away from me.' He's afraid – Jesus tells him not to be afraid, so he must have been afraid – he is afraid of this person. Think of Isaiah going into the Temple in Isaiah chapter 6. There was nothing unusual about that: but on that day in the year that King Uzziah died, he sees the Lord. The same thing happens to Isaiah. What does he do? He falls on his knees because he recognises that he is in the presence of a holy God and he is not holy. See how in that storm-moment Simon's life has been completely devastated. His perception of the teacher in his boat has been blown out of the water and replaced with the perception of God in human flesh; his perception of himself has been radically and totally transformed.

Between Jesus and himself Peter thus, and rightly, perceives a chasm – 'I can't have anything to do with you', more than that, 'you can't have anything to do with me. Look at what's wrong with me.' But, in William Cowper's words from the hymn *God moves in a mysterious way*, Jesus 'plants his footsteps in the sea and rides upon the storm'. Over this huge, real gulf that Simon only wants to widen, Jesus easily, wonderfully, graciously and purposefully reaches out. Jesus says: 'Don't be afraid. From now on you will catch men.'

Now what is, and what isn't, Jesus doing here? Jesus doesn't ask Peter to say the sinner's prayer. Jesus doesn't say 'Right! Gotcha, Simon. I want you to come to the front of the boat and give your life to me. I just want you to say this prayer after me…' Amazing, isn't it? – he hasn't even read the manual on leading sinners to Christ! Jesus doesn't even give Peter a prayer with which to climb over the chasm. He doesn't give him something to do so that he could move himself from his sinfulness over to the holiness of the Lord Jesus Christ. Jesus does the moving. Jesus reaches out to Simon and says 'Don't be afraid' (of Jesus' holiness, of his own sin, of judgement). 'From now on you'll catch men.' Jesus can get Peter over the accurately perceived gulf. Jesus can draw Peter to where he is and take the life which he has deliberately just blown apart, shattering that personal inner-world, and rebuild it, reconstructing him and recreating him to become a fisher of men.

At this point it's vital that we understand in a bit more depth how Jesus is doing all this and what he's doing beneath the surface. We have to understand something of what it meant for Jesus to be born, to live as a man, for him to die and rise again.

Jesus says that Peter will now share, participate and become a partner, in his work. He wasn't saying 'Simon, now I'm going to give you a lot of things to do. I want you to go away and do them all and then come back to me and we'll see how you've done and I'll mark your discipleship.' Jesus doesn't say 'Well Simon if you want to be a worthy sort of chap now, and if you want to stop falling on your knees and saying "I am not worthy", then these are the things that I want you to do. Successful completion of these tasks will gain you sufficient credits to stand up in front of me instead of falling at my knees.' Jesus doesn't do that kind of thing with Simon and he doesn't do that with you or me when he calls us to worship him and serve as his disciples. Why not? Because if he did we would either rightly recognise our failure at the tasks and so just collapse again, or else we would do an even worse thing: we'd come back from our errands and say: 'I've done them all – I'm pretty good at this! Now I am worthy, now I can stand before you and you're going to have to accept that you really did land a pretty good catch when you caught me.' Peter's life has been lifted onto an entirely new plane of existence – not one with failure and success as its two poles, between which the disciple will oscillate, experiencing fellowship with God at only one of them. Failure and success are still possibilities (or I wouldn't be writing this book!) but they do not define the habitat of the disciple.

Something altogether deeper than failure or success at tasks has to define Peter's new life. Simon is being called not to performance-related acceptance, but to be a partner, a participator in Jesus' own ministry. John Calvin, writing about prayer – an arena of Christian public performance if ever there was one – writes of our voices mingling with Jesus' voice before the Father's throne. Dennis Lennon, speaking once to a group of missionaries, illustrated this point by picturing a little girl going out onto the stage at Covent Garden Opera House, before a huge, knowledgeable audience and beginning to sing – falteringly, out of tune, a small, small voice. All of a sudden out of the wings comes a great opera singer – a Lesley Garrett – who stands next to the little girl. Instead of pushing the little girl aside, flicking her contemptuously off stage, she catches the little girl's tune, the real melody, and she begins to sing with her. Her small, faint voice gains confidence and strength, and to the astonishment and delight of the audience they sing a duet. It genuinely is a duet. Not one person singing it right and the other shutting up: it really is a duet for the audience's pleasure. Now that is what is happening in Peter's life. He is going to have to sing on stage but he can't sing. Yet Jesus is going to stand there with him, not pushing him aside or silencing the racket of his noisy performance; not belittling him by picking holes in his singing, or patronising him; but catching the tune, singing with him, taking up the melody of Peter's humanity and 'singing' it perfectly, drawing Peter's voice out and strengthening it, until at the end everyone has heard the most wonderful duet, and all heaven bursts into rapturous applause.

Jesus is doing the fishing and catching. He has drawn Simon over the huge chasm of his genuine unworthiness, and now, instead of giving him things to do that might make him feel even less worthy, or worse, marvellously worthy, he is saying 'Come and join me – come and sing with me! Let's work together Simon.' Jesus is the real Fisher who catches men. It's Jesus who draws people into the Kingdom; it's Jesus who transforms people's lives. And here he is drawing Simon's life up into his.

That puts our discipleship on a radically different footing, and it does it because of the incarnation – because Jesus Christ is actually among us now, by his Spirit, as one of us. How do you think of Jesus? Do you think of him as being somewhere 'up there' looking over the parapets of heaven, peering through the clouds, while you are a long way from him down here? If you feel that in your service and your worship you have to break through to Jesus, then you need to return to what the Bible teaches about Jesus Christ. He was made flesh, becoming what Paul calls the Second Adam. (Becoming what Martin Luther would later call the Proper Man.) Jesus became not just the leader of the disciples but the archetypal disciple, the real, genuine disciple of his Father. Everything he did and said was what his Father wanted him to do and had given him to say. The people that he reached were the people that his Father wanted him to reach. The people that he held on to were those that his Father had given him. Jesus' whole life, including his ministry, was one of perfect human discipleship. He is living the disciple's life, with them, among them, as one of them, and doing it perfectly. He is being the Proper Man, the proper disciple. Jesus Christ is the proper disciple for you. If you think that you are working at some considerable distance from Jesus Christ, trying to please one who is a long way off, then don't start any kind of work for Christ. If that's the way you think pull out now, because when you find the going gets too tough for you, you will realise that you have not trusted in the whole of your Saviour's person and work. You will have someone who died for you, but you won't have someone who lived for you as well. You won't have someone who knows tiredness, rejection, temptation and demands: you will not have a Saviour who is like you in every way. You will not have a Saviour who can sanctify your living. In your mind you will have someone who just died for you at the end of his life, and not someone who also lived for you, on your behalf. You won't be working with the one true Worker, you'll be working for a remote boss and your experience of discipleship will not be one of partnership and participation in Christ's work, it will be a matter of performance for an assessor.

And yet he is calling you to participate in his work. Think of it in these terms: is there such a thing as a pioneer missionary? When you go out to wherever you are sent to be his witness – the Toddler Group, the Parent-Teacher Association, the gym, the seminar, wherever – he will have been there before you. You won't be going to a place to start a work, requiring you to call him down from heaven. You won't need to pray along the lines of 'Well,

Lord, we're down here in Auchtermuchty, and we'd really like it if you would just come down and be with us.' People talk like that in churches and prayer meetings, but it's nuts! It bears no relation to the New Testament. He is there before us. He is there in Auchtermuchty before you ever reach the place. He is changing people, preparing the ground, opening doors for the gospel before you are. What he wants you to do is to join in the work that he's already started. Our praying is never a matter of overcoming divine inertia and hauling God down from heaven; it's a matter of us being called up into his work. We don't 'bring God in' on our work. We don't have to bring God in on anything! It's his world to begin with – his universe. He's the one who is working away all the time. Jesus said: 'My Father is always at his work to this very day, and I too am working' (Jn. 5:7). It's God who has to bring us in on his work. That biblical pattern gives a fundamentally different direction of movement, and a fundamentally different way of looking at ourselves, at Christ and at our service. It's our partnership with him in his work, our participation in his perfectly obedient humanity; his full, expansive, wonder-ful, funny, really 100 per cent alive humanity; his pure humanity, free from all those gnawing, nasty, rat-bag sins that pull us down.

If you approached your work in this way, you would see how that instantly takes one of the biggest sources of unconscious stress right away from Christian work. Forget all that nonsense about having to perform for the assessor. He is with you, calling you to work with him in his work. He wants you to participate in his perfect humanity and, resting in his perfect discipleship, to share in his work. He is going to be with Peter and with all the others that he will call to discipleship.

If we go back to a passage in the Old Testament that helps us to understand one of the titles of Jesus, 'Son of Man', we see the point opened up for us. In Daniel chapter 7 we have Daniel's vision of the Ancient of Days, seated on his throne of judgement with the huge crowd of saints standing in his presence and with the four beasts coming up out of the earth. Suddenly, out from among the people of God – from among the saints, who from that point on in the passage are defined as 'the people of the Most High' – comes 'one like a son of man'. He stands before the Ancient of Days as one of the people, but he comes in clouds too – a man and God. That vision of Daniel's helps to define what the New Testament means when it calls Jesus the Son of Man: he is there among you, with you as one of you, genuinely able therefore to represent you before the Father.

That day for Peter, when everything fell apart, when he suddenly realised his true identity before God, Jesus was reaching out to lift him over the chasm and say 'come and join me, come and participate in my work'.

That's the groundwork for understanding what God was doing with Peter, and for appreciating the context of his discipleship – particularly when it went wrong. That's what we're going to see again and again through the remaining chapters, but it's also why Jesus can say 'don't be afraid'. That's why Simon didn't need to be afraid, and why Jesus could say so confidently to someone who was going to prove to be a spectacular failure, 'from now on you will catch men.' Not 'you might', or 'you could', or 'you will have to try very hard to' catch men, but 'you will'. How could Jesus be so sure? Because Simon was being called to participate in Jesus' own ministry. That's what we are called to, praise God, for the rest of our lives. Not because we've just read it and understood it, but because Jesus has done it. He has, really, historically come and lived for you on your behalf. He went over the course of your humanity for you and got it right, so that he might lift us onto his level, so that our lives, our work and our service might find their purpose, meaning and even their achievement, their 'success', in his. This gives us a real hope. It gives us the very real prospect of a discipleship that can be recovered when it goes wrong, and saved from self-satisfaction and pride when it appears to be going well. It gives us the prospect of being able to understand and help those who are under a burden and a cloud, who feel that they are no use at all.

That's our call – not to a set of tasks or an expected grade of achievement: there are no performance standards being written into a contract of employment. It is a call to participate in Jesus' perfect human discipleship by the Father and so really to be a disciple. I hope that as we turn now to Simon getting it wrong, we can see the importance and also the fruitfulness of all this for him and for us.

3

The Disciple's false security

Luke 22:24-34

24 Also a dispute arose among them as to which of them was considered to be greatest.

25 Jesus said to them, "The kings of the Gentiles lord it over them; and those who exercise authority over them call themselves Benefactors.

26 But you are not to be like that. Instead, the greatest among you should be like the youngest, and the one who rules like the one who serves.

27 For who is greater, the one who is at the table or the one who serves? Is it not the one who is at the table? But I am among you as one who serves.

28 You are those who have stood by me in my trials.

29 And I confer on you a kingdom, just as my Father conferred one on me,

30 so that you may eat and drink at my table in my kingdom and sit on thrones, judging the twelve tribes of Israel.

31 "Simon, Simon, Satan has asked to sift you as wheat.

32 But I have prayed for you, Simon, that your faith may not fail. And when you have turned back, strengthen your brothers."

33 But he replied, "Lord, I am ready to go with you to prison and to death."

34 Jesus answered, "I tell you, Peter, before the cock crows today, you will deny three times that you know me."

It is said that the road to hell is paved with good intentions – but the road to many other places is similarly paved. The roads to hypocrisy, an awful lot of guilt, self-deprecation and low self-esteem in the Christian life are also paved with good intentions. Roads that lead to a lot of relational problems in marriage, at work, and in church are so paved.

Peter walked a path of discipleship with Christ that was paved with sincerely good intentions. We need to remember that Peter sincerely wanted to do the very best for Christ. We're not knocking a man who was deliberately and knowingly pretending to do the best. He really wanted to do the best in his discipleship. But he hadn't yet grasped the basis of true discipleship and, therefore, the actual basis of his present discipleship. He had yet to discover where his security in the path of walking with Christ lay; and, at least as importantly, where it did not. It's that path of sincere good intentions that we've got to remember as we see Jesus taking Peter closer and closer to the point where he's going to fail.

But there's a scene-setter that we have to pause at first. When, like Peter, we are participating in Christ's humanity, walking with him, united with him, going where he has gone, then we are going to find ourselves in the midst of conflict. We are on the side of heaven, which is being assaulted by hell; on the side of the saints, who are being assaulted by Satan; on the side of Christ who was hated and dogged by the devil. That's what participating in Christ's

humanity will necessarily involve for us. We should expect
warfare and have neither right nor reason to expect anything else in the Christian life – or at least we have no right
to expect that there will be no warfare, precisely because we
are united with Christ. His humanity, because it was completely given over to his Father, was under attack: our new
humanity, our new life, is a life that will be under attack,
suffering the assaults of hell. 'If the world hates you, keep in
mind that it hated me first,' said Jesus to the disciples
(Jn. 15:18). In prayer to his Father he said 'The world has
hated them, for they are not of the world any more than I
am of the world' (Jn. 17:14).

Somewhere in that process of attack, in a way that baffles
some of our ordinary, earthbound and faithless logic, God
allows a sifting to take place. He allows us, from time to
time, to experience the heat of the battle. Not as something
that he would rather wasn't in the Christian life, but which
is regrettably inevitable and so he'd better make the best of
it; but rather as something that is essentially a part of following him and being made like him in every respect. He
allows the sifting. Remember how God allowed Job to be
sifted? Remember how Satan came before God having
prowled to and fro through the earth? God points out his
servant Job. God knows exactly what he's doing with Job's
life: a sifting has to happen and God allows it. That's what
happens here for Peter (though for different reasons). The
heat of battle is going to do the sorting, the burning off in
Peter's life.

Peter was earmarked already for a leading role. At Peter's
confession of Christ, as Matthew records it in chapter 16 of

his gospel, we see that Jesus marks Peter out for a leading role among the disciples and the early Church. 'You are the Christ, the Son of the living God,' says Peter. Jesus, after he has said 'Blessed are you Simon son of Jonah for that was not revealed to you by flesh and blood but by my father', goes on to say 'you are Peter [*petros* – a rock] and on this rock I will build my church'. Then he says 'The keys of the Kingdom are handed over to you.'

Peter is a natural leader: always the first one to jump into anything (even the Sea of Galilee!), always the first one to get there, he's constantly ahead of the disciples – even when the rest don't want to follow! On just about every occasion where some response to Jesus comes from the disciples it's Peter who gets in there first. Sometimes he opens his mouth before his brain's in gear; or he's running before he knows what he's doing – impetuous yes, but this quality marks him out for leadership as well. He's not just appointed to it, he's actually suited to it.

In addition, Peter has seen the end point of everything. He has been encouraged by the sight of the finishing-tape. Remember when Jesus took Peter and James and John with him up onto the mountain for his transfiguration? What was happening there? Well, the Father was again, as at his baptism, authenticating Jesus before the disciples. But something was happening for the disciples as well. They were being shown a glimpse of the finishing-tape: of what Christ's glorious humanity was and therefore also what their own humanity would one day be like. As they see what awaits their Master, their Lord, their friend, they see what awaits them. As Peter caught a glimpse of the glory of God he was being shown his own destiny in Christ.

Already, then, by the time we get to Luke 22, Peter has been set up for service, leadership and responsibility – now in the Kingdom, and in the future in glory.

If Peter was going to be a rock, and one day a bearer of that kind of glory, then he needed sifting so that in the future years of service, leadership, responsibility and warfare, his faith would not fail. He needed solid ground for his discipleship. He would need to have that fundamental question of what made him feel secure clearly sorted out in his mind and woven into his deepest presuppositions about life. The sifting that Jesus was foretelling to Peter in Luke 22 concerned precisely his security.

Like Peter, we too need to grasp and understand now where our security in discipleship does and does not lie. Like Peter, we might need to be sifted. God is always preparing you for tomorrow, for tomorrow's service. None of yesterday was wasted as far as God is concerned – even the bits that you think were wasted. Look back over yesterday. Maybe you think that you wasted some of your time here and there, you were goofing around and could have been doing something better with those moments. And you are right! You could have been doing something better. But as far as God was concerned, not even those moments need be wasted: he is always preparing and teaching so that the next step can be taken that bit closer to him, and that bit more effectively for him.

Until this point in his life, Peter is on a path of discipleship which is paved with good intentions. Peter is sincere, but he is making a grave mistake. He thinks that because he is sincere, he's also secure. It's one of the biggest mistakes that we can make in our own discipleship – particularly for any involved in leadership and service who usually, by definition, are keen and sincere, and who by practice find themselves in the thick of the Christian battle with evil. Do you deeply desire to serve your Lord and do well in the Christian life; to serve effectively, to fulfil the potential which God has given you? Then you are ripe for the confusion between sincerity and security.

We know, of course, that sincerity isn't enough – you can be sincerely wrong. Peter is sincere – really sincere: it's genuine. But sincerity isn't to be confused with being secure.

Before we go on to notice more about Peter, I want to sound a word of caution about looking at where he went wrong. There is, in fact, much to admire about this man. He was through and through, totally besotted with Jesus Christ. Christ was his hero, his friend; Jesus Christ had raised his life out of nothingness and made something of him. Jesus Christ had lifted him over that sin-chasm, had picked him out, and was going to do even more with his life. And when someone does that for you, you very naturally and rightly think that they are wonderful. Peter had this wonderful heart that was captivated lock, stock and barrel by Christ. I wish that more of us were like him. We can't knock him with a smug sense of superiority.

It is the reply in v.33 that gives the whole game away for Peter. He shows what's been going on under the surface all through the three years of following Christ. 'Lord, I am ready to go with you to prison and to death.' Peter knew neither the falsity nor the irony of what he was saying. He really thought that because he was so sincerely willing, and because he could find the words to articulate his willingness, he was actually as strong and secure as he was sincere.

We can unwittingly make the same mistake. We can confuse our sincerity, and our articulated willingness, or our zeal, or our ability to understand what a speaker or an author is saying and to agree with it – we can confuse these things with our actual discipleship and its real level of security.

To make it plain our unspoken reasoning says that because *I* am sincere and keen, because *I* am understanding, because *I* am able to speak and because *I* can perform certain tasks in the Christian church; because *I* can do all these things I am therefore secure. And the word that gives the whole game away is the word 'I'.

'Lord I am ready to go with you to prison and to death!' But as the next few hours were to show so devastatingly, yet so constructively, he wasn't.

There are four things wrong. First, Peter underestimated the severity of the battle. And so can we. We underestimate just how fierce and nasty the devil is. We think he's going to fight fair and clean; a southpaw boxer maybe, but not one who'd break the rules: we're wrong. He couldn't care less about fair play. He is nasty, vicious, horrible: evil through and through. He isn't even interested in you for your own sake. He sees you only as a means of diminishing the glory of God, who is his real target. We are only of interest to him in so far as we give and reflect that glory. You're nothing to the devil in yourself. Peter had underestimated the nastiness and severity with which Satan could attack.

Second, he completely underestimated Jesus' perception of what was happening – see how he contradicts his Lord – amazing! But we do the same. This is Jesus Christ the Son of God, who knows everything, who knows the end from the beginning, whose words are wisdom itself. But Peter says to his face 'You're wrong! I'm going to follow you even to prison and I'll die for you.' He flatly contradicts the one whom he has confessed as 'The Christ, the Son of the living God.' See how bold our sincerity can make us! Not a holy, reverential boldness is it? He completely underestimates Jesus' knowledge of both him and the situation.

Third, he does some massive overestimating too. He overestimates his own courage and readiness; he also overestimates his own faith. Paul, writing to the Romans in chapter 12 urges them to have 'a sober estimate of their faith', because down here faith can be so near to pride. When we're doing well in the things of the faith – particularly in the tasks of discipleship – we start patting ourselves on the back. Our pride latches onto our faith like a leech. But if the life we lead in these earthly bodies is to be presented to God as a living sacrifice, which is our reasonable, proper way of declaring how much we think that God is worth, then we must have a sober estimate of our faith.

In his book *The Anatomy of Secret Sins*, Obadiah Sedgwick wrote: 'Believe that your own strength is not sufficient. Even the strongest ship, left to itself, cannot venture far, but it is upon the rocks and sands. Anything may prove too strong for him who conceives himself to be too strong for anything.' To put it into the context of Peter's life; don't think that you can walk on water if you can't!

Fourth, Peter was well-practised and adept at denying the things about himself that he would rather not face. We can spend a lot of time in our lives denying those things about ourselves that, for a variety of reasons, we would rather not face. We start when we are young, so that by the time we are in our twenties we are so good at it that we can do it without thinking; which is the problem. We put a lot of sub-conscious mental and nervous energy into hiding them or covering them over. (Somebody who has been doing this becomes very tired for other reasons – maybe prolonged overwork or a particularly focused and deep stress in their lives – and suddenly they don't have the energy to keep this hidden thing covered over and the cracks start appearing. And all of a sudden, at precisely the time when they are least able to cope with all this buried stuff, it all bursts out – a cesspool erupts within an exhausted soul. It may well be, of course, that some of the things hidden within us are sins which have been committed against us, in which case the pain of this moment can be even greater.)

Jesus, very graciously because he loves him so much, is forcing Peter into the situation where the covers will break open. He's going to have to face up to something that he's denying. We don't like to think of ourselves as failing our Lord – genuinely we hate the thought that we might let him down – we don't like to think of ourselves as being hypocritical, or cowardly, or as those who cop out. But we had better face up to the fact that we are well capable of being such people.

Sincerity is no ground for security because sincerity doesn't actually deal with the problems. It does not cancel out the things about ourselves that we would rather not hear about or admit. We make this classic mistake in many areas of our lives. We make the mistake with our sexuality: a man's sincerity as he makes his wedding vows won't stop him finding another woman attractive. We make the mistake with our attitudes to wealth, to other people, to aspects of our pasts, our families, our work. We become adept at denying truths in these areas that we would rather not face. Peter's sincerity not only covers an exceptionally weak position, it weakens it further because it hides the weakness.

If we think of Peter's name for a moment, and of the little pun back in Matthew 16:18 that Jesus plays on the word, which means 'rock', we can perhaps find a helpful picture for what's happening. Peter, here at the Last Supper, falsely thinks that his life of discipleship stands on the rock of his own character. What he thereby bases his walk upon is in fact as solid and reliable as a great big meringue. So, with perfect wisdom and grace, with such deep care for him, Jesus prepares Peter for the imminent collapse of the meringue; for his own fall. It has to happen.

So where do Peter's true security and strength lie? His real strength and security, the strength that he's going to need to get him through all those years of discipleship, through all those years of temptations and trials that still lie ahead of him, the strength and security that he's going to need to get to that glory that he's had a glimpse of, this real strength and security are not going to be found in Peter at

all. They are to be found only in Christ. And do you see
where it's actually found when we look at Christ? It's found
in these words: 'I have prayed for you Simon.' There, in the
Son's relationship with the Father, in the force of that word
'I' and all about Christ that is encompassed there, in the
effectiveness of the Son's praying, which lies in the quality
of the relationship with his Father; there, in *that* person,
engaged in that activity, with that other Person lies Peter's
security. We're back to that perfect discipleship of the Son
before the Father, into which we, by God's sheer grace, are
drawn by virtue of our union with the Son.

Our security lies not within us, but within that wonderful relationship between the Father and the Son through the
Spirit. Is the Father going to dismiss the Son? Neither will
he dismiss those who are united to the Son, whom the Son
in his humanity represents. Is the Son going to fall away
from the Father? Neither will those with whom the Son has
united himself fall away. In the relationship between the Son
and the Father, which makes this prayer of his for Peter
effective, lies his security, and ours.

In Hebrews 7:24 and 25 we have these words: 'He is able
to save completely [that is "to the uttermost" – as far as it is
possible to go] those who come to God through him [not
on their own!] because he always lives to intercede for
them.' I want you to be sure that I'm not making too much
out of Peter and this prayer that Jesus tells him about so
briefly. It really does have to do with more than Peter and
more than Christ's work in his life. It is a general principle
that operates in the work of Christ with his people in all
places and at all times – for you now.

So that we can understand this sifting, as well as the true and false security business a little better, let's look at what Jesus *doesn't* pray. He doesn't pray what we might be tempted to pray if we were the team leader here. He doesn't pray that Peter will be spared this trial. He doesn't say 'I've prayed that Satan won't come near you. I sent him skittling out of the heavenly courts for even daring to want to do anything with you.' He doesn't say 'I've prayed for you that you're going to have a victorious time in that court-yard, and shout 'I know Him!' and then witness successfully to the guards and the servants, twenty-eight of whom will be soundly converted', or 'I've prayed for you that no one will ask you any awkward questions in the courtyard and that you can go on thinking that you're a hero in the spiritual battle simply because you haven't actually been in it.'

Instead of these things, Jesus says, 'Simon, Simon, Satan has asked to sift you as wheat. But I have prayed for you Simon that your faith may not fail.' Jesus' prayer was simply the expression of his love for the Father.

And how was the 'not failing' going to show itself? Not by Peter being bold, strong and self-sacrificially courageous in the courtyard. Because he wasn't. Jesus couldn't have had that in mind when he was praying, because it didn't happen. So how was Peter's faith (of all things!) 'not failing' going to show itself? Well, read the next sentence: 'And when you have turned back, strengthen your brothers.' It was going to be the turning back after the triple denial that was going to represent faith not failing and be the answer to Jesus' prayer. That turning back was going to demonstrate that Jesus' relationship with his Father was the effective sure anchor for Peter.

It is an irony, strange to our neat, logic-chopping modern Christian minds, that Peter's faith not failing did not show itself in sinlessness. Jesus did not pray that Peter wouldn't sin. He was praying that Peter would turn back. And that's how we know that Jesus really did mean for Peter to go through this sifting, devastating experience. Our eyes are opened to something of the awesome and mysterious sovereignty of God here. Somehow, within his sovereignty, Christ is going to let Peter lose a battle. He's actually going to push Peter out to a point where the battle is very hot and he's going to let him lose. So that returning from this particular battle wounded, bloody, broken, utterly defeated, he can then find out how to win the war.

You see, there's a long warfare ahead of him (and us). Up until this moment Peter is in no fit state for that long warfare. Here is the first really serious onslaught in the long war. Peter thinks he's so strong that what in reality will be a battle will seem like a picnic. So Jesus has to let Peter fall to the ground, in awful defeat: it's the only way that Peter will relinquish the false and find his true security. It is the ferocity of this battle that prepares him for the long warfare.

Jesus here is not being the popular Jesus of much Christian sentiment. We are easily duped by much that passes for worship and Christian teaching into thinking that Jesus is always going to be nice and sweet and gentle with us, as if he died to cosset us in cosy fluffy nests; but he isn't, because he didn't. Our ultimate holiness and the Father's glory (and ours) are more important to him than our comfort; they were more important to him than his earthly comfort! Jesus displays with the disciples a sovereign and apparently cavalier disregard for his followers' safety, success, health, material comfort and happiness. He still regularly puts his disciples in positions where we find ourselves saying 'What on earth are you doing with me Lord?' 'Why on earth did you let me get into this situation?' 'Why did you let him be our Minister/my husband/my Dad?' (Delete or insert as appropriate!) 'What did you think you were doing God when you let that accident happen to my child?'

Jesus lets the meringue be exposed for what it is. We could change the language from cooking and battles to shepherding. We see that in his sovereignty, the Good Shepherd is allowing Peter to enter a rocky, desolate, dangerous and painful place, so that in future years such places will hold no terror, for Peter will have learned wherein his safety lies.

It has to happen; for Peter's sake and for the sake of that glory which will resound to God's praise because of Peter's life and death. And it has to *happen* to Peter. It cannot simply be a neat piece of teaching for him. It cannot simply be a clever point in a sermon. He has to experience it, to live it. His own utter inadequacy has to be etched into his being, if he is ever to experience the adequacy of Christ as the sure foundation for discipleship. And so it is for us. God doesn't just talk about this sifting – it happens. It might be happening to you. It might have been happening for some time. Maybe the maelstrom of failure, of letting Jesus down, might be just around the corner. It is a storm that certainly breaks with greater frequency than we might

imagine, for we are accustomed to hiding our failures from
each other. It's understandable: most Christians can't keep a
secret, and since much of discipleship is phrased in terms of
performance and works, rather than in terms given to us in
the huge mercy and forgiving grace of God, the last thing
you're allowed to do in churches is fail!

So Peter has to learn to trust Christ and not himself, to
be strong in Christ's strength. Do you notice how Paul
writes to the Christians in Ephesians when he writes of the
battle and the warfare? He starts the section in Ephesians 6
with these words: 'Finally, be strong in the Lord and in his
mighty power.' We hear that kind of thing from our pulpits
and platforms – it's almost become clichéd. But all the other
talk, and more perniciously, many of the unspoken messages
about living the Christian life, erode the encouragement to
trust, replacing it with the tyranny of trying harder. 'Come
to more meetings, witness to more people, read more chapters, support more missionaries, pray more with your kids.'
In the process these vital activities of fellowship, witnessing,
Bible reading, missionary support and family devotions are
reduced to drudgery. Far worse, that motivation of love to
God, which comes uniquely from resting in the grace of
God and the sufficiency of Christ's work for us, becomes
buried under the rubble of our poor performance. There are
many Christians today who live as if Paul wrote 'Be strong
in you organisational skills' (ugh!) or 'Be strong in your
zeal', or 'Be strong in the size of your church and in its
mighty reputation.' And they live like this because they have
been taught as if Paul wrote like this. But the Bible says 'Be
strong in the Lord, and in his mighty power.' It has to be the

preface for all the 'standing' that Paul will mention, and all the fighting that is implied by the need to put on armour. Only by experiencing the depths of his own weakness is Peter going to learn the depths of Christ's strength.

But there was another reason for Christ sending Peter through the storm. It had to do with the particular nature of Peter's future work. Notice what Jesus says about what Peter is to do once he has turned back. 'And when you have turned back, strengthen your brothers.' That was the ministry that lay ahead. How on earth could a man like Peter strengthen anybody in their discipleship when he was on such a weak footing himself? He couldn't. Jesus couldn't have let Peter loose with this commission without first taking Peter through the harrowing experience of seeing his own weakness, abandoning his self-security, and only then becoming strong in the Lord and in his mighty power. How could Peter be a rock for anybody as long as he was standing on a great big meringue nest? He couldn't do it. It would have been thoughtless to the point of cruelty for Jesus to have launched Peter out into a ministry for which he was hopelessly and fundamentally unprepared and unsuited. He had to take Peter through it, and he might have to take you through it, because only then will you be able to minister to the people around you. Your brothers and sisters in Christ are not there as resources on a shelf for you to take down, use, and return as you think fit. They are God's people like you, and you are there for them. What will you do when someone in your fellowship goes through major personal problems? Walk away? Turn a blind eye? Tell them you'll pray for them whilst your body language says 'get me out of here'? Or are you going to strengthen them? If you resolve to be that kind of Christian, then God will teach you, as he did Peter, about strength and security: where they don't come from and where they do come from. Jesus didn't lead Simon through the failure just for Simon's own benefit. He did it for the benefit of those to whom Simon would minister.

There is one further aspect of this prayer of Jesus. When Jesus says 'I have prayed for you', it is a man speaking who has been there already: not at the point of failure, but at the point of sifting. Jesus himself has been through hot, nasty battle. Peter was being prayed for by the perfect high priest, the perfect representative before the Father's throne, because Jesus had been there in hand-to-hand combat with the devil.

'Jesus, full of the Holy Spirit … was led by the Spirit into the desert, where for forty days he was tempted by the devil' (Lk. 4:1 and 2). The Father and the Spirit hadn't gone off-duty allowing the devil to seize his chance. It wasn't an accident. Jesus himself was led by the Spirit to be exposed by tiredness, hunger, the stresses of the elements and isolation, to the temptations of the devil, to be tempted at the points of his present human proneness – hunger, lack of influence and power. Jesus was sifted. He knew what it felt like to go through a sieve. That's why I want to emphasise that Peter's discipleship was a matter of him being united with and represented in prayer by the one who had been over the course of his humanity.

One of the early fathers of the church, Irenaeus, taught a doctrine which is normally called recapitulation. How best to interpret the word is a matter of debate, but the way that

Irenaeus thought can be described this way. In the ancient world a column of figures was added not from the top down, but literally added up, from the bottom to the top, and the total was placed at the head (cap) of the column, as the summing up of all the entries. Irenaeus talked about Christ summing up our lives; about Christ going up the column of our lives, adding experience upon experience, temptations, trials, fatigue, stress, rejection, joy and grief as he went over the course of humanity for us, as one of us in his humanity. Except that because he always put the right figure in each entry, he got the right total at the top. Left to ourselves, of course, we put in the wrong figures as we work up the column (sins here, failings there), and not surprisingly we get the wrong answer at the top. Jesus had been at those stages in the column of Peter's life that had to do with sifting, with temptation to fail his Father, with the assaults of the devil. And he got it right. So when he says 'I have prayed for you Simon', he knows what he is talking about.

He prays for you. Hebrews 7:25 again: 'Therefore he is able to save completely those who come to God through him, because he always lives to intercede for them.' It should hearten us and comfort us. It is vital for us that he prays for us. It was going to be vital for Peter.

4

The Disciple's failure

Luke 22:54-62

54 Then seizing Jesus, they led him away and took him into the house of the high priest. Peter followed at a distance.

55 But when they had kindled a fire in the middle of the courtyard and had sat down together, Peter sat down with them.

56 A servant girl saw him seated there in the firelight. She looked closely at him and said, "This man was with him."

57 But he denied it. "Woman, I don't know him," he said.

58 A little later someone else saw him and said, "You also are one of them." "Man, I am not!" Peter replied.

59 About an hour later another asserted, "Certainly this fellow was with him, for he is a Galilean."

60 Peter replied, "Man, I don't know what you're talking about!" Just as he was speaking, the cock crowed.

61 The Lord turned and looked straight at Peter. Then Peter remembered the word the Lord had spoken to him: "Before the cock crows today, you will disown me three times."

62 And he went outside and wept bitterly.

Luke describes graphically a disciplining process that Jesus must take Peter through. Of course, when I speak of discipline, I don't mean that Peter is being rapped over the knuckles for being naughty: he is being schooled. (Our English words disciple and discipline come from the same Latin word, *discipulus*, from *discere* – to learn. To follow and to learn are parts of the same process.) The writer of Hebrews speaks of this process in chapter 12:5 and 6 of his epistle. 'And you have forgotten that word of encouragement that addresses you as sons: "My son, do not make light of the Lord's discipline, and do not lose heart when he rebukes you, because the Lord disciplines those he loves, and he punishes everyone he accepts as a son." Why does he do that? The writer having quoted from Proverbs 3:12, goes on to give the purpose of this fatherly and loving correction: 'God disciplines us for our good, that we may share in his holiness.' We have been thinking in the previous chapter about what needs to be put right – Peter is going along with Christ, following Christ, but he's still not sharing in Christ's holiness – he's still doing things for God, in the sense of wanting to impress – genuinely wanting to impress – rather than finding his 'sufficiency', his sufficient holiness, in Christ and *his* holiness. What needs to be put right? What does Peter need schooling in? In abandoning self-sufficiency and self-security, and sharing in Christ's sufficiency and security, which are founded upon his holiness.

By what process did Peter fall? We've already thought of the necessity, but what of the means? I want to draw out first a very important detail about Peter in v.54, the significance of which we might easily miss. 'Peter followed at a distance.' We learn in John's gospel that one of the other disciples knows the folk who are involved in the plot to kill

Jesus and he goes in, but Peter hangs back in the courtyard. Jesus is inside, Peter stays outside. By following at a distance Peter puts himself in one of the most perilous positions for a disciple of Christ.

Consider the possibilities here. If Peter had stuck close and gone in with Jesus, he would not have had the opportunity to deny him. He would obviously and undeniably have been with Jesus: any attempt at denial would have been ridiculous. If Peter hadn't bothered going along at all, but had stayed with all the other disciples, again he wouldn't have had the opportunity to deny Jesus because no one would have been around to put him on the spot. Instead of these two options, he follows – but he does so 'at a distance'. His discipleship is close enough to separate him from those who had abandoned their Lord, but not so close that he dies to self for and with his Lord.

To be a follower of Christ, with a renewed and real humanity in Christ but then to keep a distance is perilous because we place ourselves exactly where the devil wants us. There are reasons why such a place makes us easy pickings for the enemy. Peter was keeping a distance from the one who had commanded loyalty by love. Remember how Jesus said 'Follow me' at the beginning of Peter's discipleship? The command effected the obedience. Christ's love carries its own inherent authority now, and it had done already in Peter's life. But Peter keeps away from the Lord who could safely command loyalty. Peter keeps away from the source of all real courage in the battle with Satan. He hangs back from the one who had already resisted the Tempter and who can give power against him. Peter is in a position that makes him prone to fail, jeopardised by the distance that he places between himself and his Lord.

It is so easy to follow, but to do so at a distance. To know something of Christ, to make some kind of commitment to him, but to walk with the crowd in a kind of affiliative discipleship which will not take the lonely, risky step of close and unmistakable identification with the despised and rejected Son of Man.

What does it mean? Following at a distance certainly means a lack of communication – of prayer. Not just going two or three days without a particular time of prayer. But going without that moment by moment referral to our Lord with whom we should walk closely. Following closely means that off and on through the day you constantly refer things to him. We see an item on the news, and as we sit watching the TV we turn the item into prayer; a conversation with a friend becomes a prayer; a passing ambulance prompts a quick prayer for those who are caught up in an emergency.

Peter lacked communication *from* Jesus as well as to Jesus. Jesus was at some remove across the courtyard and in a room. Peter couldn't hear the voice that had once called him; that had once said 'Come on' as Peter strained to climb out of the boat and walk on the water; that had once rescued him as he, distracted by the waves, sank to his sure death; that had once rebuked him with such pinpoint accuracy. He's away from that voice. Our listening to God is more crucial than our speaking to him. Words shape and mould us. They did when we were children and they still do. God's word re-shapes us, re-forms us, makes us what we are. The incarnate Word was making Peter what he was becoming; the written word, used by the Spirit re-makes us. His words to us are formative in a way that ours to him cannot be. We read the Bible; but are we listening? Do we pray that God, by his Spirit, will speak to us so that our Bible reading – like prayer – will be part of the constant to and fro between ourselves and God? Remember how Jesus talked and listened to his Father? Our discipleship is, in its communicative openness with God, a sharing in the communicative humanity of the Son.

But if we're keeping a distance, silent instead of prayerful, standing back from our Bibles, then we're putting ourselves in the same perilous position that Peter was in when he was in the courtyard and Jesus was in the room: not so far away as to be out of sight, but far enough away not to be able to communicate.

But it meant more than a lack of communication and close presence with Christ. It meant him putting himself close to an alien world. Notice that it means both. He is away from Christ, and in with the crowd by the fire in the courtyard. We can't blame Peter for wanting to warm himself by the fire on a cold night – that's not the point. The point has to do with his reaction to the people who are also there. Maybe he fears them, supposing them to be hostile. We do learn in John's gospel that one of the people there was a relative of the man whose ear Peter had lopped off in the garden at Jesus' arrest. Maybe it was fear of a general hostile response. Maybe the people were just curious and would have made nothing of it if he'd told the truth. Whatever the people's motives in asking Peter, it is Peter's response that is the key thing. Peter, distanced from Christ and in among the alien world, is filled with fear. Instantly we recognise ourselves. He fears their opinion; he fears the power that he imagines they have. He fears that maybe they'll do the same to him as they are doing to Jesus. When Peter's fears come to the surface we see the meringue starting to crack. His fears reveal the depths of his insecurity and weakness. The ground of his self-confidence is beginning to crumble under the weight of his fear.

It's important to recognise that for others it might crumble under other pressures. Some people's self-confidence and self-security crumbles under the weight of physical illness or depression, or sheer adversity, or incompetence – failing in areas that previously have been marked by success – or of relational breakdown. Different pressures can crush the meringue, not all of them are to do with failing Christ, but Peter's is a common one for Christians. Fear. He is too afraid to be known as a follower of Christ. It's easy when we're in a group of like-minded disciples not to be embarrassed about Christ. But when we're the only Christian in a group at work, or university, or out for an evening's socialising, don't we feel that we are going to be socially disadvantaged, shunned, taken anything but seriously, because of Christ?

It doesn't just happen in non-Christian circles. In Christian fellowship we have some strange fear of being too holy. Eavesdrop on many groups of Christians relaxing off-duty and you'll have to listen hard to hear them speaking about Christ and what he's doing in their lives. Ministers often find that even committed Christians will talk about anything other than what God is doing in their lives. In many churches it's one of the unspoken ground rules of a minister's visit or even of straightforward Christian friendship, that you shouldn't ask any spiritual questions, as if even in Christian circles there is an embarrassment about Christ. The term 'sanctificationally understated' well describes the verbal dress-code of much Christian fellowship.

Ironically, those insecurities that express themselves in fear are actually harboured and accommodated by what we think makes us secure. Somewhere inside we know that we're insecure, so we protect ourselves. We want to be thought well of, we want to be cool, we want to dress in a way that will make us acceptable to a particular group or individual. Not because acceptability will give us a greater opportunity to share the gospel, but so that we might calm the fears about what people will think of us. But fear actually exposes our self-constructed and ultimately false security for what it's been all along. Self-trust keeps Peter from throwing his whole existence in with Christ and letting Christ take care of him. He thinks that he can take better care of himself than Christ can. Nahum Tate closes his hymn *Through all the changing scenes of life* with this verse: 'Fear him ye saints, and you will then have nothing else to fear; make you his service your delight, he'll make your wants his care.' In reverence, awe and profound respect for his loving, sovereign power and his willingness to exert it for you, throw your lot in with him. Lean upon the perfect, representative humanity, upon the offering of that humanity in your place on the cross, of that perfection being made over to you there. Trust him completely; stick close to this person who is your whole reason for being, and he'll look after you. Peter needn't have worried about what might have happened to him, he needn't have worried about what they could do to him, because Jesus never forsakes the soul that trusts in him, even if it had meant Peter going to a cross. Fear him and then you will have nothing else to fear, 'make you his service your delight, he'll make your wants his care' – and he can look after them better than we can.

The fear and insecurity are being exposed. He follows Christ from a distance, just where Satan wants him. So that all it takes is really just a gentle nudge – all it takes is three simple questions from total strangers without warning. Three prongs probing the same weakness; three little stabs which have a devastating effect on Peter, cornering him into deeper self-despair. He who had said 'You are the Christ, the son of the living God' finds himself now uttering these words of denial. As we read the accounts of how Peter replies to these questions more and more stridently we catch that Peter realises that he is falling fast – he is plummeting and he knows it. There is a deepening despair and self-loathing. First time: 'I don't know him.' Second time he's getting worse – defensive, more emphatic: 'I do not know him.' In Matthew's gospel we read that by the third time – about an hour later (what an hour that must have been) – he is swearing and cursing and calling down curses on himself and the others. We learn from Luke's gospel that he spits out vehement, expletive denials and cries out 'Man, I don't know what you're talking about!'

And he hears it coming out of his own mouth. Sometimes when we sin we know that we're doing something desperately wrong, we can hardly believe that we're doing it, but we still go on doing it. Part against our will, part compliant, we've boarded a runaway train from hell that spirals back down there. He isn't just crumbling, he is being pulled down. Then with the last words out of his mouth, the cock crows.

Do you see how much he is denying? He has walked with Christ, laughed with him, eaten with him, marvelled at him, worshipped him. His whole life has been transformed by Christ. He has been rescued spiritually and physically by Christ. He has had time spent on him by the eternal Son of God. He has been prayed for – and he's screaming 'I don't know him!'

But it isn't yet enough. Something else happens. Up until now, Peter is appalled at himself, dismayed and despairing. He is going down fast, but so far he is assessing himself. Something else has to happen, and it happens in what must be one of the most dramatic moments in the whole of Scripture, save the cross itself. The cock crows. Across the courtyard, from inside a room where he is surrounded by vicious, barking dogs, being tried, interrogated, falsely accused, harangued towards crucifixion yet bearing all with perfect control, a man is thinking of Peter. Not one thing has happened that is beyond the ken of Jesus. Not one moment has passed without the perfect awareness of the Saviour comprehending its significance for Peter. He knows where Peter is, what he's been doing. Staggeringly, he is more concerned with Peter at that moment when the cock crows than he is with himself. All the hateful noise going on in front of him fades into a silent background. And in that moment of suspended animation, the all-gracious, all-wise one 'turned and looked straight at Peter'. Luke uses a particular verb, it means a close look, a penetrating, piercing look that sees to the very heart of a man. You may have seen the film *Robin Hood, Prince of Thieves* with Kevin Costner. There is a moment in the final battle scene at the castle in Nottingham when Robin Hood's newly discovered younger brother is about to be beheaded. The tension builds as the executioner raises his axe; in that split-second when it is about to fall Kevin Costner, across the courtyard, sees the moment, comprehends the danger, and in one sweeping movement pulls a cloth-wrapped arrow from his quiver, ignites the tip, and looses it through the melée, across the battle-strewn chaotic courtyard. The camera sits on the arrow as it flies straight and true; the peripheral action falls away left and right; the target comes nearer and nearer, the axe-man grows larger and larger filling the screen for a frame; the arrow strikes him dead.

Like that arrow, Jesus' look flew swift, straight and true. Loosed with split-second timing it hit its target and penetrated even the self-absorbed remorse of Peter's desperation.

Until that moment he has been his own judge – he is appalled at himself for failing under his own standard. But that look full of compassion, truthfulness, shared pain, loving judgement, needing no words to steer it to Peter's heart – that look finally slays him. It was bad enough a second before, but that look from his hero, friend, Lord, brings him to bitter tears and, as Mark tells, breaks him down. This big man's whole world fell apart. Because of that ruthlessly loving look.

Now this is something about the love of God that we need to grasp. There is a relentless severity about his mercy, a clarity of purpose about his transforming grace that will not be distracted. If you follow him with all your heart, he will have you right, though it pain you enormously. It sounds inconceivable in these self-sensitive days when therapy must glow pleasantly, but like a surgeon, Jesus would rather hurt you to have you well, than gently indulge you as you sink into a spiritual coma. He is more concerned that you 'share his holiness' than that you have a good time. His love is so much better, more thorough, more persevering, more purposeful than what we often call love. Those he loves he disciplines. Holy love had to be ruthless. Peter had to know that he had really let not himself but Christ down. Peter had to see that he did not have the security and strength to do anything for Christ. What he was going to need for all those future years of ministry was Christ's strength. If we can say this about the self-determining, omnipotent God, Jesus *had* to look then at Peter. He had to fire the arrow that would slay the flesh, the self-trust, impetuous confidence, self-grounded boldness. He had to loose that look and break Peter down. The necessity came from within his holiness and love.

Before Peter's discipleship could ever be built on solid rock; before ever this Simon could become truly 'for others', a Peter, a rock; before ever he could reach out his hand to those who were sinking as he had once had a hand stretched out to him; before ever he could galvanise lives around the love of God as his once had been galvanised; before ever he was going to speak the truth in Spirit-given courage rather than flesh-inspired boldness in front of the same assembly that tried Christ that night and made Peter so afraid, Jesus had to slay him, to crush the false foundation for his discipleship and ground it on himself.

These days, few will tell us these things. There is little in our shallow, cost-free, feel-good gatherings that we call church to prepare us for when it all goes wrong. But it's somewhere that I've been. Illness crumbled the meringue for me. On 17 August 1981, I was in an industrial accident at the light engineers where I had a summer job as a student. The muscles down my back were ripped and I was taken into hospital in excruciating pain. The cursory visual check-over failed to detect a disc injury. When I was discharged from hospital I was given some exercises for the muscles and the disc tore again. I had to withdraw from my University course and resign as President of the Christian Union. Just about every activity had to cease. I could make no contribution and relied entirely on friends. I felt like a burden, getting in the way, and a depression ensued which took me about eighteen months to get over. It was an intensely painful experience, in more ways than one. Everything that was going well came apart, for my deep-seated, growing self-confidence had to crumble. I thank God for it to this day.

Your God is Peter's God. The one whose holiness you are called to share is this one who slew the sin and self in Peter because he had something so much better for him. He may well do that with you. You might not see it coming. It may come in an area of your life where you think you have no problems; in fact it will probably have to come in such an area. God's grace, and in all likelihood the temptation, will take you on your blind side where you have assumed that you are secure. That's what our Lord did with Peter. Peter was broken down by the devil who asked to sift him as wheat; broken down, by his own fear that revealed his completely inadequate self-sufficiency; broken down by the fact that he was never really participating in Christ but still thinking that he could impress him and do things for him in an independent sort of way; but ultimately, finally, he was broken down by his Lord. We do not have a sugary, sweet, soft, marshmallow Lord. It's idolatry to think that we do. We craft an idol out of our own desire for nice feelings; an indulgent God who only ever makes us feel warm and cosy, a fluffy, divine comfort blanket. If we've been duped into imagining that kind of God, then we are in for a shock. We will not be able to cope with the real world activity of our God. Much of Scripture will make no sense and be no help. We will neither know him nor glorify him for who he is. We will construct a 'Christian life', an experience of church, a mish-mash of spiritual clichés; we will seek out or create utterly self-absorbed worship, safe, non-challenging fellowships, Christian huddles that are designed – perhaps subconsciously, though I doubt that it is entirely so – not to enhance our holiness or to glorify God, but to justify, protect and enhance our comfort-zone. I believe that we are doing this very thing in the evangelical church today.

The real God will take us through the painful process of ceasing from self and forsaking our indulgent idols, so that we might trust and genuinely participate in his humanity. Self-enhanced and indulged humanity is not what God has in mind for his loved ones. He will wound us in order to heal us. He will allow us to be sifted.

5

The Disciple's path back

John 21:1-14

1 Afterwards Jesus appeared again to his disciples, by the Sea of Tiberias. It happened this way:

2 Simon Peter, Thomas (called Didymus), Nathanael from Cana in Galilee, the sons of Zebedee, and two other disciples were together.

3 "I'm going out to fish," Simon Peter told them, and they said, "We'll go with you." So they went out and got into the boat, but that night they caught nothing.

4 Early in the morning, Jesus stood on the shore, but the disciples did not realise that it was Jesus.

5 He called out to them, "Friends, haven't you any fish?" "No," they answered.

6 He said, "Throw your net on the right side of the boat and you will find some." When they did, they were unable to haul the net in because of the large number of fish.

7 Then the disciple whom Jesus loved said to Peter, "It is the Lord!" As soon as Simon Peter heard him say, "It is the Lord," he wrapped his outer garment around him (for he had taken it off) and jumped into the water.

8 The other disciples followed in the boat, towing the net full of fish, for they were not far from shore, about a hundred yards.

9 When they landed, they saw a fire of burning coals there with fish on it, and some bread.

10 Jesus said to them, "Bring some of the fish you have just caught."

11 Simon Peter climbed aboard and dragged the net ashore. It was full of large fish, 153, but even with so many the net was not torn.

12 Jesus said to them, "Come and have breakfast." None of the disciples dared ask him, "Who are you?" They knew it was the Lord.

13 Jesus came, took the bread and gave it to them, and did the same with the fish.

14 This was now the third time Jesus appeared to his disciples after he was raised from the dead.

Peter's story doesn't end in the courtyard. He wasn't left in a ruined heap. There was a path back. We might think that Peter's reinstatement comes from v. 15 onwards, and that these first 14 verses simply set the scene for us. So why are we stopping the momentum of denial and restoration to take note of these first 14 verses? Something vital is happening that leads to Peter being reinstated. God is doing for Peter what he often does for us: when people become Christians, when the Lord is reinstating us. Often it's without us being aware of what's going on; it might happen over many years or months, or in minutes. What's happening is that Jesus is paving the way for Peter to return. He is removing obstacles and laying down stepping stones on which Peter can come back to discipleship, a better kind of discipleship than he had before.

New houses are being built near where we stay. At the moment you can work out where the walls are going to be from the foundations and from a few courses of blocks that have been laid. (The rooms look awfully small for the price!) The rest of the building site is a complete mess – rubble, mud, debris all over the place. It's extremely unlikely that the property developer who is building these houses is going to sell any of them if the area is going to be left a mess, albeit with a few nice houses in the middle. All the rubble and debris will have to be cleared away and then they will still have to build roads, lay paths and plant gardens before anyone can move in. That's what Jesus is doing here. He is clearing away the debris of disobedience, all the rubble of offence and guilt, that there was after the denial – clearing away the rubbish and laying down a path so that Peter can actually come back to real discipleship.

Jesus is wonderfully kind that he should make it easy for Peter to return. He is in the superior position; he has the high moral ground. Peter is the worm, who has failed. Jesus could very easily have made Peter carry on squirming for a while. But he doesn't. He scores no points in their relationship. The look in the courtyard was enough. No more pain is needed; he has wounded in order to heal – now comes the healing. Jesus has never stopped being kind and gracious. How good Jesus is with us: he whom we offend when we sin makes it easy for us to return. He whom we grieve paves the way for us to enjoy the forgiveness and restoration that we need and with which his love blesses us.

Four paving stones are laid on once rubble-strewn ground. The first is so simple that we are prone to miss it.

It's almost so simple that I'm a little embarrassed at mentioning it – but it's usually the simple obvious things that we miss, because we tend not to read the words carefully. The first thing is that he goes to where Peter is: to Galilee. Peter has gone back home, to familiar surroundings. You can almost imagine the things that would go through Peter's mind that would send him back home 'What was I doing in Jerusalem anyway – what was I doing, a fisherman, a northerner down there in the sophisticated south, dazzled by all these amazing buildings, my jaw dropping like a country bumpkin's?' So he's gone back to a safe place, familiar accents, homely surroundings. He's gone back to fishing. 'What was I doing being a disciple for these three years, what was I playing at, what fantasy land was I living in?' He would be lashing himself with self-disillusionment and remorse. Despondent, he's gone back to doing what he knows best, he's gone back to doing the safe, familiar thing – he's gone back to the boat and, literally, gone fishing. 'I'm going out to fish,' Simon Peter told the rest of the disciples, snapping himself and them out of the glums.

Fishing for fish, though; not for men any more. Fishing for self; not for Jesus' kingdom. This is a reversal of what Jesus had called him to. Simon Peter has turned the clock back in his life to the time before not only his failure, but also before he was involved in the enjoyable and successful enterprise that had gone so painfully wrong. The others are there too. It's just like the whole thing had never happened, only there's the pain to live with.

So what does Jesus do? Does he sit down south in Jerusalem at headquarters? Christ behind a desk, impatiently drumming his fingers and asking, 'Where are they? They should be here. Are they letting me down again? Where's their commitment?' No. Jesus goes to where Peter is. Jesus can understand the pain, the need for a safe place. He can find Peter when Peter isn't even looking for him.

Jesus meets us exactly where we are. We noticed that he did just that at the very beginning of Peter's discipleship. He met him just where he was – at the point of futile toil, of pointless labour, in Luke 5. Well now, after the years of seemingly futile discipleship, after what must have seemed to Peter to be a pointless three years, Jesus goes to meet him where he is. He gets down with him when he's down. Not standing over him and sticking in the spiritual boot. Not crowing over him saying, 'I told you so.' The devil does that – the devil will make you squirm, the devil will kick you when you're down, the devil will pile guilt upon guilt, reminding you again of past failings that you know are forgiven, dredging up old sins that you'd forgotten about because they were dealt with and you'd moved on. But God never will. If the story of Peter teaches us anything at all, it should teach us, for our reassurance and for the comfort of our souls, that when we are down in the depths, even when God has placed us there, he gets down into the mire with us to lift us out. He has the grace to handle the truth properly and he has the truthfulness to deploy the grace constructively. Truth and grace had pierced Peter's heart like an arrow. Now grace and truth are as swift to follow. Peter needed healing.

You see how we are brought right back to the incarnation, where we started: to the real context for our discipleship. We are right back to Jesus assuming and taking upon himself our humanity. He knows what it's like. We might say that Jesus doesn't in fact know what it's like to fail God, to sin and let the Father down. So what use is his incarnate humanity at this point? But Jesus does know. He has assumed Peter's sin and ours on the cross. Do we think that he didn't feel their horror, and the horror of being away from the Father? But if we're going to pursue the fact of Jesus bearing sin on the cross, then we have to say – with praise in our hearts – that he doesn't just know what sin is like; he knows what *your* sin is like, for he carried the burden of it on the cross. Assuming your humanity, and on the cross assuming all its sin, he is able as the mediator in heaven to know what precisely your particular shape, size, colour, hue, texture of sin is. And he knows it because he has carried it. What a complete Saviour we have in Jesus Christ!

The fact that Jesus goes to where Peter is gives us hope as we pray for evangelism. Jesus still goes where sinners are: we don't have to 'bring him in' from a distance, persuading him against his better judgement to meet with these reprobate pagans at the bar or in the boardroom. Some of our praying reflects such a misconception: we speak as if we've got to inform God about a situation before we can pray about it. 'Lord, thou hast doubtless read in this morning's papers …' Give him the facts and then follow through with the requests. If we don't give him the facts, remembering to mention the absolutely crucial bit, then the requests aren't going to make much sense to him. But we don't need to do that. We should assume, when we are praying for family, friends, colleagues, neighbours, even total strangers, that

Jesus already knows absolutely everything about the person we're praying for. He even knows which bit is the crucial one! So our praying needs to change from the 'Let me update you here Lord so that you'll see why we want to come in on the situation in this particular way', to 'Lord, you know everything about this, bring me in on it, bring me up to speed on things, help me to catch up with where you are so that I can be of some help to these people and truly serve you here.' It should give us hope to know that Jesus has got there ahead of us and is already aware of everything about a situation, and wants to do something even more than we do. We should pray more confidently for people. In reality, there's no absolutely pioneering mission; there's no absolutely pioneering praying either.

Second, Jesus reminds Peter of the first lake-side call. You can see the echoes here of Luke 5. Another spectacularly useless night's fishing has been endured. (It really must have got Peter down – he failed at fishing when Jesus first called him, then he failed at discipleship, now he's gone back to fishing and he's failing at that again). God is at work behind the scenes again. Was it an accident that there were no fish near the boat that night? Was the Trinity making the most of a happy coincidence in the morning? Never! Could a God who is omniscient, omnipresent and omnipotent, who can so deftly work with split-second timing in people's lives, who sustains the whole universe by the very power of his word, have forgotten about Galilee? Even if he were forgetful, would he have forgotten that the Son was there that morning for a fairly important working breakfast, to restore Peter for all that planned and promised ministry? It does seem a tad unlikely, doesn't it! It was all meant. It was another *kairos* moment when God was at work to bring events together again for Peter.

Jesus stands on the shore. He calls out to them and they don't recognise him – it's early morning and they have been up all night, the light is not good, they are about a hundred yards from the shore. He calls out to them: 'Friends, haven't you any fish?' 'No,' they answer, bouncing the shout off the water back to the shore. Jesus says 'Throw your net out on the right side of the boat.' Why did he say the right side? Why not just, 'Throw your net over the side again'? Why did he want them to throw it over on that side and not the left side? Isn't it because the same omnipotence, which had withheld fish all night long – hiding them from these professional fishermen – was now bringing a whole shoal of them up alongside the right side of the boat?

They throw the net out and surprise, surprise; it's another miraculous catch of fish. Are the lights beginning to go on in Peter's mind yet? They have certainly gone on in John's mind. As the truth spreads in John's mind, with lightning speed through his memory, his intelligence, his awareness, he says to Peter (good work, John, thinking of Peter just then), 'It is the Lord.' Not 'the Master' of Luke 5:5, but the 'Lord' of Luke 5:8. And just like Peter the eager disciple once did – not Peter the failure – he reacts by leaping over the side and wading to the shore, taking time only to grab his coat!

Now what does it say to us as we watch it happen? It says that Jesus is still the same Jesus. The action says 'Remember when I overcame the futility of your unsuccessful work?

Remember when I overcame the chasm of your unworthiness? Remember when I overcame the pointlessness and self-centredness of your life and called you to be a partner with me? Well, I'm still the same me.' Jesus takes Peter back to those first few moments when grace became known to him. He does that with you and me too. When the blessedness of 'the hour I first believed' has gone, chased off by temptation, weariness, or failure, he takes me back to that hour, to its blessedness and its truth. He takes me back to that evening in June 1973 in Bradford City football ground when I went forward after the evangelist Arthur Blessit had preached the gospel; when his grace got me out of my seat and won my heart.

Third: he is taking Peter back to those moments of his own response. Jesus is re-triggering the joy and wonder at the grace of God, that first heart-burst towards the Saviour. He takes Peter back to the time when there were no eggshells to tread on, to that immediate, spontaneously childlike response that was so typically Peter's.

Jesus isn't doing this for his own sake, but for Peter's. Peter doesn't just need to see and experience the same, faithful grace of God again. Peter needs also to experience again his own responsive heart. Peter needs to be able to say to himself 'Yes! I'm being happy again – because of Jesus!' Peter needs to see his own muscles obeying, following, working towards Christ again. He needs to see that he's not wiped out by sin, that he can respond again. He needs that level of evidence to counter the devil's lie that he is down and out. We need to see the evidence in our own lives that God has, in the language of Isaiah 42:3, which Matthew picks up to

describe Jesus (Mt. 12:15ff.), not snuffed out the smouldering wick or broken the bruised reed. The devil tells us that
he has, whispering to us that God – our God – has snuffed
out the prospect of any God-honouring, fruitful, enjoyable
discipleship; has snapped the bruised reed. But Jesus, wisely
and graciously, at just the pace that we can take, gently fans
us back into flame again so that we feel again both the
warmth of his love, and the warmth of our own revived,
answering devotion. Jesus – such a wonderful pastor – knew
that Peter needed the encouragement of seeing that yes, he
could do it again. With profound awareness of fine details of
Peter's life, he supplies the grace that courses through even
the tiny capillaries of Peter's complex personality.

Jesus lays the fourth paving stone by doing something
clever, imaginative, creative and down to earth. He does
something kind and practical. He gets breakfast ready.
The fire is already going. The fish are already there. The
disciples are tired after a night on the lake. It was an
eminently sensible thing to do. It was also a loving thing to
do – to anticipate the need and respond with appropriate
action. It wasn't a sermon that these men were ready for, nor
a seminar, nor a few songs and a Bible study. They needed
food. The Jesus who understands the fine details of your
inner life, also understands when you're hungry! But more,
the Jesus who understands your need for truth and grace
also understands that kindness touches and wins hearts.

We need to show more of that kindness in our churches
and in our evangelism. I need to show more of it. If you
want street-kids in Lima to understand love, you show them
love. You show them that there are adults who won't rip

them off, or turn them into child prostitutes and drug dealers, or make them disappear. You show them love, and then they can understand when you talk about a God who loves them. Same for your friend in suburbia: business-woman, mother, wife, daughter, stressed-out, in need of the love of God. Show her his love; don't talk about it yet.

Jesus shows it to Peter at the lake shore that morning by making breakfast. Simple. Too simple for some of us clever Christians. But not too simple for the Son of God. Jesus uses the kind deed to lay the fourth paving stone for Peter's return to himself, and Peter's renewal in discipleship. He does it in a lovely way, that echoes the whole point about participative discipleship. Look closely at what's written, because while we don't want to strain the text, we have to recognise that every word is vitally important. There are no casual details, no redundant phrases stuffed in to pad out an otherwise thin storyline. Every word and every detail count. Jesus has a fire going and fish on it; so what does he ask the disciples to do? 'Bring some of the fish you have just caught.' Hang on a minute: Jesus has already got fish on the fire. What's he doing? Is he playing silly games with the disciples?

No, he's doing several things. First, he's triggering more of the typically wholehearted, one hundred and ten per cent Peter-ish response. Peter goes down to the boat and he hauls the whole net up the shore! 'You want fish, Lord? Here's 153 big ones!' For goodness sake! How is Jesus going to fit 153 big fish on a little fire? Were they going to eat 153 for breakfast? (Did Peter stop to think of that? I'm glad he didn't.) But Peter's smouldering wick is being fanned back into flame – this really is the same Peter who once wanted to climb out of a boat onto a storm-tossed lake at night in order to walk on the water towards Jesus!

But by asking them for some of their fish, he's also reminding Peter that what Peter was called into was partnership. Jesus could have impressed them with a virtuoso display of fishmongering, dazzled them with culinary mastery. Jesus could have had a barbecue with a full breakfast at the mere snap of a finger. But he doesn't. Instead he puts some fish there and then says 'I'd like your fish too.' It's a delicate, deft and beautiful reminder from Jesus that he wants Peter to be a partner, a co-worker in the task of fishing for more disciples.

Do you think that Jesus couldn't do spectacular things all on his own in your town, among your colleagues and neighbours, with your friends? Couldn't he turn on a virtuoso display of evangelism? Of course he could! But he wants your partnership.

There's one other statement being made by the action here. Jesus is giving the early church a reminder of that church act which most reminds us of the partnership. They are having communion. There on the beach. Communion hasn't been refined yet into a carefully formal, or just as carefully informal, church ceremony, but that's what they are doing. He wants them to have communion with him, just as he still invites us to gather around his table with him and take the bread and wine (juice?) into our bodies, assimilating them, them and us become one.

Without Peter realising how it's done, he is participating again, back having a meal with his friend. He is won back from the depths of his own despair. Love has healed him from those wounds which love had caused. Jesus has won Peter back, and is about to set his feet on a solid rock. Jesus has done what Psalm 40 talks about. He has reached down, lifted Peter out of the 'miry clay', set his feet upon a rock, and put a new song in his mouth. What a kind and wise Saviour. Hallelujah!

6

The Disciple re-calibrated

John 21:15-17

15 When they had finished eating, Jesus said to Simon Peter, "Simon son of John, do you truly love me more than these?" "Yes, Lord," he said, "you know that I love you." Jesus said, "Feed my lambs."

16 Again Jesus said, "Simon son of John, do you truly love me?" He answered, "Yes, Lord, you know that I love you." Jesus said, "Take care of my sheep."

17 The third time he said to him, "Simon son of John, do you love me?" Peter was hurt because Jesus asked him the third time, "Do you love me?" He said, "Lord, you know all things; you know that I love you." Jesus said, "Feed my sheep.

Well, breakfast is over, friendship has been shared, Peter has the big grin all over is face. We might look at that picture and see a happy scene of fellowship between Jesus and these men, a 'happy band' of brothers. But appearances can deceive. We've followed the story closely, and taken careful note of the depths of offence that Peter caused and the depths to which he sank as a result of failing his Lord and friend. We know that despite the appearances, there's still something to be dealt with that morning. So far Jesus has only cleared the rubble away and paved the way for Peter to be brought back into full, free and deep fellowship with him.

When I take wedding services, I ask if anyone knows 'any reason why the bride and groom may not lawfully be joined together in marriage'. The old form of words referred to 'any just impediment'. There is still a just impediment, an obstacle, a certain matter to be raised. Everyone there knew about it; most importantly, Peter and Jesus knew about it. Was it going to be ignored, like the proverbial elephant in the room? Or would it be raised and dealt with? There was unfinished business in Peter's life. It is a sign of the Good Shepherd's wisdom, kindness and grace that he draws Peter aside and walks along the shore, away from the rest of the disciples. (Note that Jesus isn't interested in a public flogging.) Just the two of them, to finish this emotional, spiritual business. It really is a sign of the perfect pastor's care that he does this with Peter, even though Peter may have guessed what was coming and quietly dreaded it. For this particular unfinished business would have ruined Peter's life and crippled his service, hamstrung him in his discipleship. Peter absolutely has to have the business finished. Remember here that the context for discipleship is not one of being operatives in God's business; the context is that of being united with Christ in his humanity as well as in his death and resurrection: partnership with him in his perfect following of, and living with, the Father. The unfinished business isn't really, at heart, a matter of Peter's effectiveness at the tasks, it is a matter of the fellowship, the partnership, the relationship between them.

That's how it is in any working relationship. When you're having to work with people, the tasks are one thing, but the key to the work is the relationship – how you're getting on. How much more in a relationship within a family, or within a church. If there's bad air between people, the communication doesn't go so well, the helpful little touches are missing, the considerate anticipation of needs never happens, the thoughtful additions to the basic requirements which make all the difference are never made. It's the relational element in the partnership that needs sorting, not a glitch in the system.

In his pastoring of Peter Jesus neither writes him off for being a failure, nor lets him off as if the offence didn't matter. With perfect grace he addresses the problem. Remember how Jesus went to where Peter was and met him again at the point of his failure? We need to remember that when God, in his infinite mercy, comes to us where we are he also, in that same mercy, doesn't leave us where we are. He will always be taking us forward, always leading us into greater likeness to Christ. That's what we mean by Jesus re-calibrating Peter.

The battery in my watch ran out recently. The watch has served me well for many years, but the battery went. I could have written the watch off: thrown it away and bought a new one. Or I could have said 'Oh that doesn't matter – it still looks like a fine watch; no one will notice that it's not telling the right time any more, I'll just wear it anyway.' But neither option would do. (I can't afford a new watch that often, and the second option would be stupid.) I had to get a battery put into it. Putting the battery back in was, in a sense, what was happening to Peter in the last chapter.

But when the new battery was put into my watch, the watch was still telling the wrong time. The jeweller had to re-calibrate my watch so that it told the right time. It's not enough just to be repaired a bit. You need to be reset so that you measure up to the only accurate disciple. That's what I mean by re-calibrating.

My particular job in that light engineering firm in Aberdeen was servicing pressure gauges that came in from the oil rigs. Out there they were treated less than delicately. They came back in a real mess. I had to turn them round and get them back out again. They looked fine after they'd been serviced, repainted and polished. But they weren't ready to go back out – until they'd been re-calibrated against the standard. Jesus is re-calibrating Peter against his perfect humanity, his true discipleship.

There are three parts to the process. Each is vital, and you may be able to identify the way they have worked together in your own life.

The first is that he asks the question. Jesus asks, 'Do you love me?' I want you to imagine that you are a failed Christian in a church. You've really sinned in a major way. (Yes, that Harvey Wallbanger stunt at last night's house group was just one too many for the humourless elder who happened to come along.) How would you be treated by the Christians around you, and even perhaps by your pastor? I suspect that in many churches you might be treated in exactly the way that Jesus does *not* treat Peter here. Jesus doesn't say 'Peter, what on earth made you say

that? What on earth made you do that?' which is what a lot
of church leaders or other Christians would ask. (The question mark is redundant: it's not really a question that you're
being asked!) Jesus doesn't embark on an adversarial, accu-
satory analysis of what Peter did. Peter was wounded
enough by the look that Jesus gave across the courtyard.

Jesus doesn't say what our evangelical sub-culture would
suggest, nor does he say the things which our common and
hopelessly misconceived approach to discipleship would
suggest. Jesus doesn't say 'Will you try harder next time?'
Trying harder is not the key to discipleship. Putting in more
effort, doing more things, running faster, spending more
time doing the religious stuff, all this is not the crux of the
matter. Of course, laziness is no virtue, neither is casual,
careless discipleship. Yet there are so many broken Christians
who feel as if they have the rest of their Christian world –
certainly their leaders – shouting 'Try harder. Do more. Be
better.' You might as well stand over a bird with a broken
wing and shout 'Flap harder!' It cannot flap harder, and the
one shouting is worse than ineffective. Jesus doesn't say 'Try
harder next time.' Neither does Jesus make Peter squirm:
'Don't you feel miserable, Peter? Don't you see before your
very eyes the heinous and exceeding sinfulness of your sin,
Peter? Don't you see the depths of your misery?' Nor, does
Jesus say 'Peter, you'll be okay if I hear a good repentance
from you – so come on: a good, thorough, well-phrased
repentance with all the key words to get the formula right,
and the right tone of voice.' Yet that is effectively the position that many wounded, broken Christians find themselves
in. They have been taught a picture of God as one who

demands an adequate repentance. Some, with more than a touch of residual pride, think that they can repent well enough. Repentance becomes a work of the flesh – a sufficient cause of God's forgiveness: salvation by good-enough repentance. Troubled and scripture-sensitive souls will ask 'Have I repented well enough? What if I forgot a sin, or didn't realise all the facets of a sinful action? What if my motives were impure? What if my very repentance is itself something that needs repenting of? What if my repentance is tainted with the same sinfulness as the sin that I'm repenting of?' The path of adequate repentance is a never-ending spiral down, away from God.

Until, of course, one is turned around by the truth of Christ's grace. For he is the Proper Man, he is our righteousness. Christ's repentance, as one of us, covers ours. When he was baptized by John with that baptism of repentance in the Jordan, he got down into the river along with everyone else to identify himself with us in our need to repent. He even, nay especially, did *that* for us. It's crucial that he did that much for us, or our repentance would never have been assumed by him and never redeemed by him. Our repentance would never be redeemed from its feebleness, its inevitable selfishness, its woefully inadequate view of the heinous and exceeding sinfulness of our sin and of the pure holiness of God. So Jesus Christ repented for us   to give us real repentance. He hasn't helped us by providing his people with a magic formula that, if followed, will deliver the required forgiveness. We don't find 'Ten Steps to Perfect Repentance' in the Bible. Jesus didn't do anything that would make repentance our work over which our ceaseless pride could boast. Instead he, having taken our humanity, did it for us so that we, by virtue of our union with him, can trust him – with faith that gives glory to God, not with works that give glory to us – even in this matter of repentance. And all our imperfect repentance he took upon himself on the cross.

It is unfortunate, to say the least, that we live in a church that has been so infected by the world, with leaders who have themselves laboured under a works-dominated view of discipleship. We have developed a sub-culture of works which inevitably breeds either despair or self-confidence.

So what is the question that Jesus asks? He simply says 'Do you love me?' He goes back to what had failed in the courtyard. Underneath the fear and cowardice, the failure of confidence, boldness or courage, lay the failure of Peter's love. Love ventures; when we love, we commit security, happiness, well-being, the future, to the one loved. Love failed that night. It was weakened, thoroughly human love that failed to show love's courage, love's close loyalty, love's obedience.

It would, of course, be love that would be needed in the future, when continuing, enduring discipleship with Christ would make the ultimate demand upon Peter; when he would be bound hand and foot and martyred. More than raw courage would be needed then. Nothing less than love would do.

We are reminded again that at the heart of being with God is not successful performance, but a relationship of love. We have to get straight that love is the crucial thing in discipleship. It is what God wants from us. Believe it or not,

God doesn't actually need an extra pair of hands! He isn't short of bright ideas, nor of strength, nor of creative power. It's not our accomplished performance at certain good works that he sent his Son to redeem. It's us he wants – to love us and to receive from us answering love. Such love, and nothing less, will yield all our giftedness to him. It will motivate wholehearted and costly service, 'obedience glad and true'.

Love is what he *commands* from us. That sounds strange to us – to command love. Of course, *we* can't command people to love us – and a good thing too! We sometimes wish we could. We perhaps wish that we could make some-one love us because we think we love them. But God *does* command love. What did Jesus teach in Matthew 22:37 and 38, quoting Deuteronomy 6:5? 'Love the Lord your God with all your heart and with all your soul and with all your mind. This is the first and greatest *commandment*' [my italics]. God doesn't suggest love as some sort of optional extra, to be added on to an otherwise successful discipleship. It is the very essence of following him, and he commands it as of first importance.

But love isn't just what he wants from us, or what he commands: it's also what he gives us. Another of the early church fathers, Augustine, had this short prayer: 'Command what you will and give what you command.' And it has to be like that, for we are disabled by our sin from giving him anything that he commands. But when he commands, he gives the power to obey the command.

Two incidents in the gospels illustrate the point. Along comes a man with a withered hand, asking Jesus to heal him. What does Jesus command? 'Stretch out your hand.' He tells him to do the one thing that he can't do. But with the command comes the ability. There are the mourners outside the tomb of Lazarus, that prison-cell of death. What does Jesus, his heart heaving with the most profound grief, do? He talks to a dead man, commanding him, insisting that he walk. 'Lazarus, come out of there.' With the command comes the power to obey, and Lazarus walks. God commands love from us. We can't do it ourselves. We are by nature at enmity with God: in love with ourselves and with sin. Yet God commands that we love him; and what he commands he gives.

So Jesus goes to the very heart of the matter, which is the state of Peter's heart. He questions Peter about his love for him – not asking because he doubts that it's there, but because he is looking for the love that he has given to emerge.

The first part in the process of re-calibration is that particular question. The second part is the answer: 'Yes, Lord, I do.' As Peter needed to see his own responsiveness to Jesus earlier that morning, so Peter needs to hear his love expressed on his own lips. He needs to hear the words of love that will ease the painful acid-burns of those words of denial. From this moment he will be able to remember *these* words coming out: 'Yes, I love you.' The file that contained the denials is now being overwritten with the file that contains 'I love you.' It is vital that Peter hears it for himself - much more important than that the one who knows Peter's heart anyway should hear it. See how wise and loving a physician of souls we have in Jesus. Battle-scarred, sin-stained Peter is drawn out to say emphatically 'Lord, you know that I love you' – to protest not, this time, his ignorance of Jesus, but his love for him.

We do a pretty good job, with the devil's help, of writing ourselves off. We kick ourselves when we're down; we have learned to do it when we are young. Many of us have picked up from the world, or our parents or siblings or at school, that we are sub-standard. So we adopt that position in life. We need to be reminded by the physician of our souls, when we have fallen, that the love which he has placed in us – a love for himself, has not been eradicated by our sin. It is actually true that where sin abounds, his grace abounds more. We need to be reminded that we really are a new creation, that underneath the failure and the wrecked meringue nest of our own security or self-confidence, lies the love of God – love that he has given us, in Jesus Christ. That's what Jesus is doing here. He's taking Peter back to that moment when after the futile night's fishing, he first saw the Lord and followed him. But he's taking him also to a new depth within himself. Peter now finds that God has planted, deep and sure in his soul, a love for God.

It can be an immense relief to learn that though we sin God's grace abounds. However far we fall, God has done a work which goes deeper. Even though we go to the very bottom of the slimiest pit of sin, we find that our Lord has already been there, has taken the sin, has redeemed the humanity that lurked there, has provided righteousness for us in himself, has provided a rightness of relating to the Father that includes love. When you sink to the darkest and vilest depths of your own soul, what do you find? You find

Jesus the Proper Man, with a perfect love for the Father. You actually are redeemed from the depths, for you are a partner with him in loving the Father.

Then comes the third element of Peter's re-calibration: his re-commissioning. After each 'I love you', comes the command – 'Feed my lambs – take care of my sheep.' He gives him work to do again. And once more, we cannot get away from the fact that Jesus is calling Peter to be a partner in his own work – just as he called him in fisherman's language in their first encounter. Think of it. Who is the good shepherd? Who calls his sheep by name? Who really knows where good pastures are to be found? Who can find lost sheep and pick them up again? Peter? No, Jesus. Now Jesus calls Peter into the same line of work. What a relief it must have been to Peter in years to come to be able to say that Jesus had asked him, three times there and then, to shepherd his sheep and thereby share in Jesus' work.

It's so important that Jesus, right then, affirms Peter's usefulness and genuine partnership in his work. We grow up gaining the idea that our identity and worth come from our work. I used to think that this was a particularly male thing, since when men cannot work any more, we very often go downhill rapidly. It's a real problem for many men facing retirement. They know that a fortnight after they've left work, they'll hardly be missed. And what sort of a contribution to the world is going for the paper and some milk in the morning? Ask most men what they are and they'll give you their job title! But it's not just a retired male thing. Irrespective of age or gender, it's a terrible thing to think that for all your gifts and experience, you're regarded as useless. It can be crushing, especially for those who lack confidence, who have been bashed around by life, or who habitually compare themselves unfavourably with others, to have their conscientious contribution criticised. We have to take a great deal of care and thought to make sure that we do it constructively, if we're going to do it at all in our churches. If you can't speak the truth in love, don't speak.

Look at what Jesus, who knows a thing or two about perfection, says and doesn't say. Not only does he refrain from saying how useless Peter is, he deliberately takes Peter aside to affirm Peter's place in his work. In fact Jesus is reaffirming what he had once promised to Peter, which is important. Jesus says 'after you have come back, strengthen your brothers', itself an echo of what we have in Matthew 16, 'You are Peter and on this rock I will build my church.' There was work to be done in the Kingdom, work to be done in a partnership which Jesus had chosen for nobody but Peter, and which had been promised to nobody but Peter. Peter's willingness, his courage, his over-the-edge-of-the-boat-and-into-the-stormy-water-zeal, were just what God had made, so that exactly this Peter could do the work given to him. Peter's appearance, speech, style, and now especially this experience that he had been taken through, were just what God wanted. Is it by accident that you live where you do, look like you do, have your particular sense of humour? Was the Divine Designer of the entire universe, who can time shoals of fish swimming round boats in Galilee to perfection, somehow absent when key events or decisions which affect your life were made? Does the sovereignty of God not extend as far as your living room, or solicitor's office, or gene pool?

That never means that we are inevitably successful in the world's terms, or that we are going to have an easy life. God's sovereignty means that there might be huge and agonising problems to go through. But it also means that these dark times are a part of fitting the uniquely shaped characters that the infinitely creative God has made into the uniquely shaped niches which he has made for us.

By the end of breakfast the work in Peter's life was done. All that had been accomplished would soon lead to that energising moment, another great turning moment in the history of redemption, when the Spirit descended. Peter would stand before those who had filled him with fear that night in the courtyard and boldly declare the name of Jesus. He would be imprisoned rather than disown his Lord. He would see the commanding promises – to be a fisherman and a shepherd in Christ – come to fruition. He would become in Christ what Christ had called him to be.

★ ★ ★

Like countless Christians after him, Peter was taken through the dark turmoil of failing his Lord. It was the only way for Peter to learn that being a disciple meant living on an entirely different foundation from the one that he had lived on before the great fisher of souls caught him. Failure was the way to begin building on the foundation of life in Christ. It was for Peter the door to hope.

Even though we limp and stumble as we walk with him, and we will always walk with at least a limp down here, it is this future of partnership with Jesus Christ that keeps us sane and gives us hope when discipleship goes wrong. Being united with the one who has lived with God aright for us, who has carried all our sins and infirmities for us by his death, who has given us eternal life in his resurrection, is the only basis for enduring. Jesus himself is our hope; not his gifts nor his blessings, and certainly not our successes, but he himself. Our whole discipleship, our 'humanity with God', is summed up in that one name, Jesus.

To the glory of God, which is where the glory belongs.

Appendix

New Testament references for being 'in Christ'

John 14:20 On that day you will realize that I am in my Father, and you are **in me**, and I am in you

John 15:2 He cuts off every branch **in me** that bears no fruit, while every branch that does bear fruit he prunes so that it will be even more fruitful.

John 15:4 Remain **in me**, and I will remain in you. No branch can bear fruit by itself; it must remain in the vine. Neither can you bear fruit unless you remain **in me**.

John 15:5 "I am the vine; you are the branches. If a man remains **in me** and I in him, he will bear much fruit; apart from me you can do nothing.

John 15:6 If anyone does not remain **in me**, he is like a branch that is thrown away and withers; such branches are picked up, thrown into the fire and burned.

John 15:7 If you remain **in me** and my words remain in you, ask whatever you wish, and it will be given you.

John 16:33 I have told you these things, so that **in me** you may have peace. In this world you will have trouble. But take heart! I have overcome the world.

Acts 4:2 They were greatly disturbed because the apostles were teaching the people and proclaiming **in Jesus** the resurrection of the dead.

Acts 17:28 `For **in him** we live and move and have our being.' As some of your own poets have said, `We are his offspring.'

Acts 26:18 ... so that they may receive forgiveness of sins and a place among those who are sanctified by faith **in me**.

Romans 6:11 In the same way, count yourselves dead to sin but alive to God **in Christ** Jesus.

Romans 6:23 For the wages of sin is death, but the gift of God is eternal life **in Christ** Jesus our Lord.

Romans 8:1 Therefore, there is now no condemnation for those who are **in Christ** Jesus,

Romans 9:1 I speak the truth **in Christ** – I am not lying, my conscience confirms it in the Holy Spirit –

Romans 12:5 so **in Christ** we who are many form one body, and each member belongs to all the others.

Romans 14:14 As one who is **in the Lord** Jesus, I am fully convinced that no food is unclean in itself. But if anyone regards something as unclean, then for him it is unclean.

Romans 16:3 Greet Priscilla and Aquila, my fellow-workers **in Christ** Jesus.

Romans 16:7 Greet Andronicus and Junias, my relatives who have been in prison with me. They are outstanding among the apostles, and they were **in Christ** before I was.

Romans 16:8 Greet Ampliatus, whom I love **in the Lord**.

Romans 16:9 Greet Urbanus, our fellow-worker **in Christ**, and my dear friend Stachys.

Romans 16:10 Greet Apelles, tested and approved **in Christ**. Greet those who belong to the household of Aristobulus

Romans 16:11 Greet Herodion, my relative. Greet those in the household of Narcissus who are **in the Lord**.

Romans 16:12 Greet Tryphena and Tryphosa, those women who work hard **in the Lord**. Greet my dear friend Persis, another woman who has worked very hard **in the Lord**.

Romans 16:13 Greet Rufus, chosen **in the Lord**, and his mother, who has been a mother to me, too.

Romans 16:22 I, Tertius, who wrote down this letter, greet you **in the Lord**.

1 Corinthians 1:2 To the church of God in Corinth, to those sanctified **in Christ** Jesus and called to be holy, together with all those everywhere who call on the name of our Lord Jesus Christ – their Lord and ours:

1 Corinthians 1:4 I always thank God for you because of his grace given you **in Christ** Jesus.

1 Corinthians 1:5 For **in him** you have been enriched in every way – in all your speaking and in all your knowledge –

1 Corinthians 1:30 It is because of him that you are **in Christ** Jesus, who has become for us wisdom from God – that is, our righteousness, holiness and redemption

1 Corinthians 3:1 Brothers, I could not address you as spiritual but as worldly – mere infants **in Christ**.

1 Corinthians 4:10 We are fools for Christ, but you are so wise **in Christ**! We are weak, but you are strong! You are honoured, we are dishonoured!

1 Corinthians 4:15 Even though you have ten thousand guardians **in Christ**, you do not have many fathers, for **in Christ** Jesus I became your father through the Gospel.

1 Corinthians 4:17 For this reason I am sending to you Timothy, my son whom I love, who is faithful in the Lord. He will remind you of my way of life **in Christ** Jesus, which agrees with what I teach everywhere in every church.

1 Corinthians 9:2 Even though I may not be an apostle to others, surely I am to you! For you are the seal of my apostleship **in the Lord**.

1 Corinthians 11:11 **In the Lord**, however, woman is not independent of man, nor is man independent of woman.

1 Corinthians 15:18 Then those also who have fallen asleep **in Christ** are lost.

1 Corinthians 15:22 For as in Adam all die, so **in Christ** all will be made alive.

1 Corinthians 15:31 I die every day – I mean that, brothers – just as surely as I glory over you **in Christ** Jesus our Lord.

1 Corinthians 15:58 Therefore, my dear brothers, stand firm. Let nothing move you. Always give yourselves fully to the work of the Lord, because you know that your labour **in the Lord** is not in vain.

1 Corinthians 16:24 My love to all of you **in Christ** Jesus. Amen.

2 Corinthians 1:20 For no matter how many promises God has made, they are "Yes" **in Christ**. And so through him the "Amen" is spoken by us to the glory of God.

2 Corinthians 1:21 Now it is God who makes both us and you stand firm **in Christ**. He anointed us,

2 Corinthians 2:14 But thanks be to God, who always leads us in triumphal procession **in Christ** and through us spreads everywhere the fragrance of the knowledge of him.

2 Corinthians 2:17 Unlike so many, we do not peddle the word of God for profit. On the contrary, **in Christ** we speak before God with sincerity, like men sent from God.

2 Corinthians 3:14 But their minds were made dull, for to this day the same veil remains when the old covenant is read. It has not been removed, because only **in Christ** is it taken away.

2 Corinthians 5:19 that God was reconciling the world to himself **in Christ**, not counting men's sins against them. And he has committed to us the message of reconciliation.

2 Corinthians 5:21 God made him who had no sin to be sin for us, so that **in him** we might become the righteousness of God.

2 Corinthians 12:2 I know a man **in Christ** who fourteen years ago was caught up to the third heaven. Whether it was in the body or out of the body I do not know – God knows.

2 Corinthians 12:19 Have you been thinking all along that we have been defending ourselves to you? We have been speaking in the sight of God as those **in Christ**; and everything we do, dear friends, is for your strengthening.

2 Corinthians 13:4 For to be sure, he was crucified in weakness, yet he lives by God's power. Likewise, we are weak **in him**, yet by God's power we will live with him to serve you.

Galatians 1:22 I was personally unknown to the churches of Judea that are **in Christ**.

Galatians 2:4 *This matter arose* because some false brothers had infiltrated our ranks to spy on the freedom we have **in Christ** Jesus and to make us slaves.

Galatians 2:17 If, while we seek to be justified **in Christ**, it becomes evident that we ourselves are sinners, does that mean that Christ promotes sin? Absolutely not!

Galatians 3:28 There is neither Jew nor Greek, slave nor free, male nor female, for you are all one **in Christ** Jesus.

Galatians 5:6 For **in Christ** Jesus neither circumcision nor uncircumcision has any value. The only thing that counts is faith expressing itself through love.

Ephesians 1:1 Paul, an apostle of Christ Jesus by the will of God, To the saints in Ephesus, the faithful **in Christ** Jesus:

Ephesians 1:3 Praise be to the God and Father of our Lord Jesus Christ, who has blessed us in the heavenly realms with every spiritual blessing **in Christ**.

Ephesians 1:4 For he chose us **in him** before the creation of the world to be holy and blameless in his sight. In love

Ephesians 1:7 **In him** we have redemption through his blood, the forgiveness of sins, in accordance with the riches of God's grace.

Ephesians 1:9 And he made known to us the mystery of his will according to his good pleasure, which he purposed **in Christ**.

Ephesians 1:11 **In him** we were also chosen, having been predestined according to the plan of him who works out everything in conformity with the purpose of his will,

Ephesians 1:13 And you also were included **in Christ** when you heard the word of truth, the gospel of your salvation. Having believed, you were marked in him with a seal, the promised Holy Spirit,

Ephesians 2:6 And God raised us up with Christ and seated us with him in the heavenly realms **in Christ** Jesus,

Ephesians 2:7 in order that in the coming ages he might show the incomparable riches of his grace, expressed in his kindness to us **in Christ** Jesus.

Ephesians 2:10 For we are God's workmanship, created **in Christ** Jesus to do good works, which God prepared in advance for us to do.

Ephesians 2:13 But now **in Christ** Jesus you who once were far away have been brought near through the blood of Christ.

Ephesians 2:22 And **in him** you too are being built together to become a dwelling in which God lives by his Spirit.

Ephesians 3:6 This mystery is that through the gospel the Gentiles are heirs together with Israel, members together of one body, and sharers together in the promise **in Christ** Jesus.

Ephesians 3:12 **In him** and through faith **in him** we may approach God with freedom and confidence.

Ephesians 4:21 Surely you heard of him and were taught **in him** in accordance with the truth that is in Jesus.

Ephesians 5:8 For you were once darkness, but now you are light **in the Lord**. Live as children of light

Ephesians 6:10 Finally, be strong **in the Lord** and in his mighty power.

Ephesians 6:21 Tychicus, the dear brother and faithful servant **in the Lord**, will tell you everything, so that you also may know how I am and what I am doing.

Philippians 1:1 Paul and Timothy, servants of Christ Jesus, To all the saints **in Christ** Jesus at Philippi, together with the overseers and deacons:

Philippians 1:14 Because of my chains, most of the brothers **in the Lord** have been encouraged to speak the word of God more courageously and fearlessly.

Philippians 3:9 and be found **in him**, not having a right-eousness of my own that comes from the law, but that which is through faith in Christ – the righteousness that comes from God and is by faith.

Philippians 4:1 Therefore, my brothers, you whom I love and long for, my joy and crown, that is how you should stand firm **in the Lord**, dear friends!

Philippians 4:7 And the peace of God, which transcends all understanding, will guard your hearts and your minds **in Christ** Jesus.

Philippians 4:21 Greet all the saints **in Christ** Jesus. The brothers who are with me send greetings.

Colossians 1:2 To the holy and faithful brothers **in Christ** at Colosse: Grace and peace to you from God our Father.

Colossians 1:14 **in whom** we have redemption, the for-giveness of sins.

Colossians 1:17 He is before all things, and **in him** all things hold together.

Colossians 1:19 For God was pleased to have all his fulness dwell **in him**,

Colossians 1:28 We proclaim him, admonishing and teach-ing everyone with all wisdom, so that we may present everyone perfect **in Christ**.

Colossians 2:6 So then, just as you received Christ Jesus as Lord, continue to live **in him**,

Colossians 2:7 rooted and built up **in him**, strengthened in the faith as you were taught, and overflowing with thankfulness.

Colossians 2:10 and you have been given fulness **in Christ**, who is the Head over every power and authority.

Colossians 2:11 **In him** you were also circumcised, in the putting off of the sinful nature, not with a circumcision done by the hands of men but with the circumcision done by Christ,

Colossians 3:18 Wives, submit to your husbands, as is fitting **in the Lord**.

Colossians 4:7 Tychicus will tell you all the news about me. He is a dear brother, a faithful minister and fellow-servant **in the Lord**.

Colossians 4:17 Tell Archippus: "See to it that you complete the work you have received **in the Lord**."

1 Thessalonians 2:14 For you, brothers, became imitators of God's churches in Judea, which are **in Christ** Jesus: You suffered from your own countrymen the same things those churches suffered from the Jews,

1 Thessalonians 3:8 For now we really live, since you are standing firm **in the Lord**.

1 Thessalonians 4:16 For the Lord himself will come down from heaven, with a loud command, with the voice of the archangel and with the trumpet call of God, and the dead **in Christ** will rise first.

1 Thessalonians 5:18 give thanks in all circumstances, for this is God's will for you **in Christ** Jesus.

2 Thessalonians 1:12 We pray this so that the name of our Lord Jesus may be glorified in you, and you **in him**, according to the grace of our God and the Lord Jesus Christ.

1 Timothy 1:14 The grace of our Lord was poured out on me abundantly, along with the faith and love that are **in Christ** Jesus.

2 Timothy 1:9 who has saved us and called us to a holy life – not because of anything we have done but because of his own purpose and grace. This grace was given us **in Christ** Jesus before the beginning of time,

2 Timothy 3:12 In fact, everyone who wants to live a godly life **in Christ** Jesus will be persecuted,

Philemon 1:6 I pray that you may be active in sharing your faith, so that you will have a full understanding of every good thing we have **in Christ**.

Philemon 1:20 I do wish, brother, that I may have some benefit from you in the Lord; refresh my heart **in Christ**.

Philemon 1:16 no longer as a slave, but better than a slave, as a dear brother. He is very dear to me but even dearer to you, both as a man and as a brother **in the Lord**.

Philemon 1:23 Epaphras, my fellow-prisoner **in Christ** Jesus, sends you greetings.

Hebrews 3:14 We have come to share **in Christ** if we hold firmly till the end the confidence we had at first.

1 Peter 3:16 keeping a clear conscience, so that those who speak maliciously against your good behaviour **in Christ** may be ashamed of their slander.

1 Peter 5:10 And the God of all grace, who called you to his eternal glory **in Christ**, after you have suffered a little while, will himself restore you and make you strong, firm and steadfast.

1 Peter 5:14 Greet one another with a kiss of love. Peace to all of you who are **in Christ**.

1 John 2:5 But if anyone obeys his word, God's love is truly made complete **in him**. This is how we know we are **in him**:

1 John 2:6 Whoever claims to live **in him** must walk as Jesus did.

1 John 2:28 And now, dear children, continue **in him**, so that when he appears we may be confident and unashamed before him at his coming.

1 John 3:6 No-one who lives **in him** keeps on sinning. No-one who continues to sin has either seen him or known him.

1 John 3:24 Those who obey his commands live **in him**, and he in them. And this is how we know that he lives in us: We know it by the Spirit he gave us.

1 John 5:20 We know also that the Son of God has come and has given us understanding, so that we may know him who is true. And we are **in him** who is true – even in his Son Jesus Christ. He is the true God and eternal life.

Revelation 1:9 I, John, your brother and companion in the suffering and kingdom and patient endurance that are ours **in Jesus**, was on the island of Patmos because of the word of God and the testimony of Jesus.

Revelation 14:13 Then I heard a voice from heaven say, "Write: Blessed are the dead who die **in the Lord** from now on." "Yes," says the Spirit, "they will rest from their labour, for their deeds will follow them."

Christian Focus Publications

Our mission statement –

STAYING FAITHFUL

In dependence upon God we seek to impact the world through literature faithful to His infallible Word, the Bible. Our aim is to ensure that the Lord Jesus Christ is presented as the only hope to obtain forgiveness of sin, live a useful life and look forward to heaven with Him.

Our Books are published in four imprints:

CHRISTIAN
FOCUS

popular works including biographies, commentaries, basic doctrine and Christian living.

CHRISTIAN
HERITAGE

books representing some of the best material from the rich heritage of the church.

MENTOR

books written at a level suitable for Bible College and seminary students, pastors, and other serious readers. The imprint includes commentaries, doctrinal studies, examination of current issues and church history.

CF4•K

children's books for quality Bible teaching and for all age groups: Sunday school curriculum, puzzle and activity books; personal and family devotional titles, biographies and inspirational stories – because you are never too young to know Jesus!

Christian Focus Publications Ltd,
Geanies House, Fearn, Ross-shire,
IV20 1TW, Scotland, United Kingdom.
www.christianfocus.com